DOIN' THE CHARLESTON

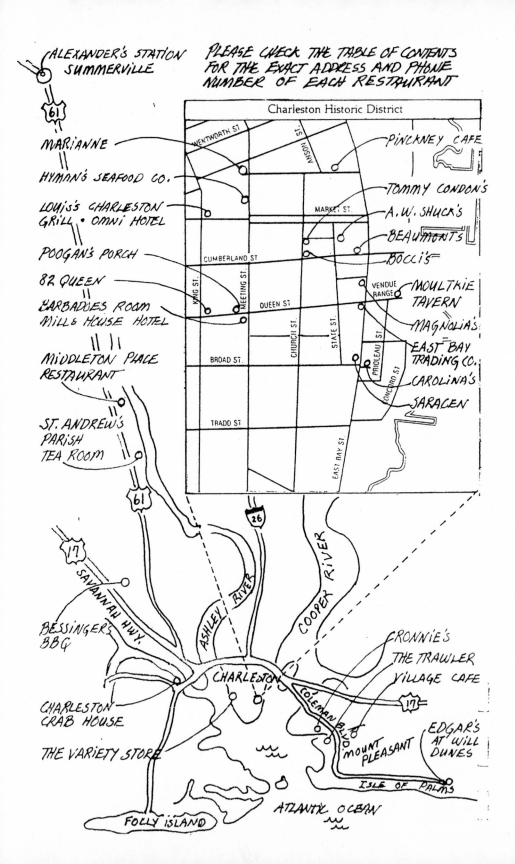

Doin'

The

Charleston

By Molly Heady Sillers

Edited by Tia Sillers-Purcell
Food Editor, Helen Marie Cunningham
Illustrated by Robert Sillers

Southern genre artist and friend Samuel Ravenal Gaillard sketched and painted all of the following works included in this book: pages 37, 77, 83, 95, 105, 120, 122, 129, 153, 159 plus this charming lady who appears striding across many of the recipes.

Sixth Printing   May 1995

Book designed by
ROBERT   SILLERS

To the treasure that is friendship,
the comfort of family,
the heritage of tradition,
the continuity of the generations,
the love of all creatures,
the joy of laughter,
the thrill of being alive,
the pleasure of the garden,
and the wonder of all God's Creation!

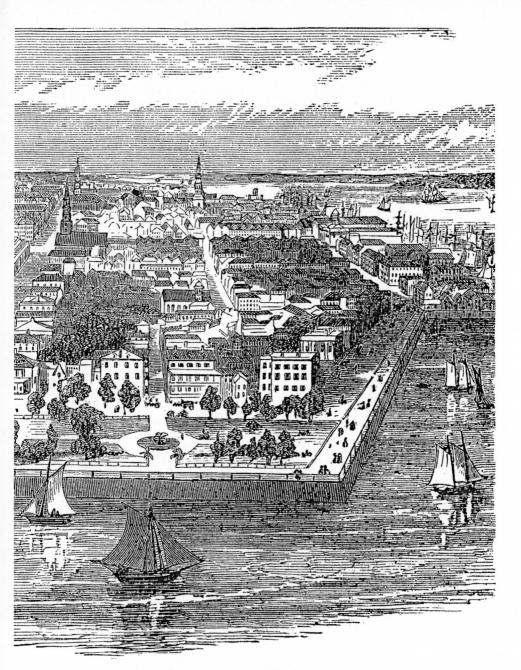

A birds' eye view of Charleston, May 1862

🦐 INTRODUCTION 🦐

The purpose of this book is to direct you to the best restaurants in Charleston and allow you to recreate the recipes they are known for! Charleston's cuisine has a character all its own. Many early Charlestonians were Englishmen who first settled plantations in Barbadoes. When they came to Charleston, they brought with them Barbadian touches and the island foods. Add to this the heritage of the African cooks who brought okra, many greens, yams and sesame seeds; and the cookery of the French Huguenots, all blended in a colonial pot.

The cuisine of the South Carolina coast is termed Lowcountry. The name is rooted in the geography of the region. The Lowcountry is that continuous stretch of land scarcely above sea level that starts with the Atlantic Ocean lapping its shores and reaches inland for many miles. A world of sea islands, marshes, estuaries, rivers, bays and creeks, the Lowcountry is held captive by the rhythm of the tidewaters across this coastal plain, and is teeming with life.

Rice is used abundantly as it has been since the beginning of plantation days when a sea captain brought the first seeds. It brought wealth to Charleston and was called "Carolina Gold." The seafood is as fresh as the latest catch! The small farms of the sea islands provide a bountiful harvest of vegetables and fruits evidenced by the hand-lettered signs along the road to Kiawah.

For a city its size, the number of excellent restaurants is second to none. In the historic area, many are a leisurely walk from the best hotels, quaint bed and breakfast inns and historical points of interest. Going over one of the many bridges, one restaurant is perched on a creek lined with a whole shrimping fleet at its back door. Another greets sailors who come by yacht! Take your pick of Irish pub, traditional French, bistro, Italian trattoria, Greek, Thai, Nouveau South, or even a Confederate tavern! Have no doubt that this port city has it all.

A real live Porgy courted a real live Bess here! A wild, loose-jointed dance came off the shipping wharfs and started a craze. This is home to people of humor: Early Charlestonians enjoyed a "laughing club" where nothing serious could be discussed, and one club promised a speaker every 100 years! The hardest task in writing this guide to Charleston, was to remind myself that it is a cookbook and guide to the city's best restaurants and not a love letter to the city itself!

If Charleston has the mellowed romantic appeal of a European city, it's no wonder. It was one of British America's first planned cities under Charles II. The settlement called Charles Towne was planned around 1673 complete with two main streets and over 375 lots! A large score of the existing homes are pre-Revolutionary and many are of national importance. The city has survived fires, tornadoes, earthquakes, and hurricanes to become a treasure-trove of architectual heritage.

Geography shaped Charleston's history. The harbor brought the first ships to this point. Framed by two rivers, the setting was ideal as rivers were the highways of the times. The first settlement was up a protected river. It was this strategically placed peninsula that cast the vote to build the permanent town here. What a perfect vantage point to view the harbor and ready a defense. The early Englishmen who came here via Barbadoes chose Charleston because of its geography. Water is a pivotal part of the cultivation of rice. The plantations along the Ashley and Cooper rivers could be flooded through dikes to create the perfect fertile environment for a flourishing plantation.

The Charleston perspective is rooted in geography and the love of place. There's a certain egocentric view of reality; everything is centered on the Charleston vantage point. Charlestonians stand in awe at this alter of God's creation. It *is* the "Holy City," and the sacredness is in the geography. The peninsula of Charleston lies like a jewel in a crown studded with sea islands and rivers. Any native will tell you Charleston lies "where the Ashley and the Cooper rivers meet to form the Atlantic ocean."

Legend: 2. Ashley River 3. Charleston 6.Castle Pinckney 7. Fort Ripley
8. Fort Johnson (James's Island) 11. Fort Moultrie 12. Battery Gregg
(Cummings Point) 13. Fort Wagner 14. General Gilmore's Advanced
Batteries 18. Iron-clads and Wooden Ships. 19. Hotel.   July 1863

Charleston has seen the vicissitudes of life and weathered them. From 1695, it flourished as a rice culture, shipping more barrels of rice to Europe than any other source. In the Revolution, the Tories sacked it. After the Revolution, the invention of the cotton gin made growing cotton profitable and indigo was another strong crop. The wealthy planters built many a High Battery mansion along White Point Gardens. Over twenty wharfs and many warehouses thrived in antebellum Charleston.

The Civil War brought this civilization to its knees and left a fragmented, struggling South. Disuse and ruin were prevalent, as the agricultural economy fell apart. Charleston learned to make do. With the advent of World War II, commerce finally revived allowing the city to become a major shipbuilder, port and naval base.

Through thrift, tenacity and pride Charleston has prevailed. The preservation owes a lot to this combination of deprivation coupled with an intrepid spirit. The "too poor to paint; too proud to whitewash" attitude saved an intact architectural legacy. A major force was an emerging group which came about in 1920 and later became the Preservation Society of Charleston. In addition, Charleston was the first city to pass a historical zoning ordinance. In 1931, the City Council adopted a proposal outlining the 144 acre, Old and Historic District. It is to the credit of the Preservation Society that even with the new growth and vitality, it is still a low rise city with no building higher than its steeples!

This is a city where remodeling is a word abhorred; where renovation raises eyebrows; where restoration is viewed with reservation, and preservation alone is sacrosanct. Everyone you turn to can identify Greek Revival, French, Regency and Italianate architecture. They can inform you as to Corithian, cornice, cornerstone, cobblestone, and keystone. And as for those under-roof, open-air rooms; In Savannah, they're verandahs; throughout the South, they are much loved porches; but in Charleston alone, they are piazzas (pe-at´zas). Most anyone will be hospitable in explaining.

Charlestonians have a tradition of aristocratic manners and unfailing politeness. The arts are another cherished tradition. The Dock Street Theater is the oldest in the country. There is an appreciation of artisan and artifact, weavers and weaving, artists and art. Museums and art galleries abound. The Spoleto Festival, an event of opera, dance, theater, jazz and visual arts is spread out all around the city and has fostered a cultural renaissance.

The tour of the harbor will stir your romantic imagination as will the famous gardens and plantations. Outstanding too, is Charleston Landing dating to 1670; Fort Sumter, where the Civil War began; and the retired Yorktown aircraft carrier is part of the new Naval and Maritime Museum. Plantation scenes from *Gone With The Wind* were filmed here at Boone Hall!

January brings the camellia tours at Magnolia, Middleton, and Cypress gardens; February has the Southeast Wildlife Festival; and March hosts the Candlelight tour at Drayton Hall. March and April celebrate the Festival of House and Garden. The last week of May - first week of June brings the Spoleto Festival; September and October celebrate the Fall House and Garden Tour; November brings Plantation Days at Middleton, as well as the Charleston Regatta, a rowing race held on the Ashley River.

Charleston is home to 181 churches, and many toll their bells on the hour. Charleston is ancient live oak trees, yellow jessamine, magnolias in sequestered gardens, the sound of horses hoofs over cobblestone streets and the lyrical voices of the "flower ladies." It is the street cries of the colorful street venders calling SHEEEEEE-Crab and a hundred other delights, not the least of which is a dazzling choice of where to eat! Rhett Butler knew what he was talking about when he told Scarlet he was "going back to Charleston -- back where I belong." My bet is that he came back to enjoy some mighty fine dinin'. Bon appetit!

····◆·─◆◯◖ CONTENTS ◗◯◖─◆····

Page

Alexander's Station................................14
116 Main Street, Summerville, S.C. (803) 875-1100

A.W.Shuck's Oyster Bar...........................20
70 State Street (803) 723-1151

Barbadoes Room of the Mills House Hotel...............24
Corner of Meeting and Queen Streets (803) 577-2400

Beaumont's Restaurant Charleston...................30
12 Cumberland Street (803) 577-5500

Bessinger's Bar-B-Que & Buffeteria.................36
1602 Savannah Hwy. 17 S. (803) 556-1354

Bocci's..40
158 Church Street (803) 720-2121

Carolina's.....................................44
10 Exchange Place (803) 724-3800

Charleston Crab House............................52
145 Wappoo Creek Drive (803) 795-1963

East Bay Trading Co..............................56
Corner of East Bay and Queen Streets (803) 722-0722

Edgar's at Wild Dunes Resort......................60
Isle of Palms, S.C. (803) 886-2299

Eighty Two Queen................................64
82 Queen Street (803) 722-4428

Hyman's Seafood Company Restaurant................72
213 Meeting Street (803) 723-6000

Louis's Charleston Grill..........................74
The Omni Hotel, 224 King Street (803) 577-4522

Magnolia's.....................................80
185 East Bay Street at Lodge Alley (803) 577-7771

Marianne...88
235 Meeting Street (803) 722-7196

Middleton Place Restaurant.......................................96
Hwy. 61, Ashley River Road (803) 556-6020

Moultrie Tavern...106
18 Vendue Range (803) 723-1862

Pinckney Cafe...112
18 Pinckney Street (803) 577-0961

Poogan's Porch...116
72 Queen Street (803) 577-2337

Ronnie's...122
Shem Creek & Hwy. 17, Mt. Pleasant, S.C. (803) 884-4074

Saracen..126
141 East Bay Street (803) 723-6242

St. Andrew's Parish Tea Room..................................132
Hwy. 61, Ashley River Road (803) 766-1541

Tommy Condon's..138
160 Church Street (803) 577-3818

The Trawler...142
Hwy. 17 at Shem Creek, Mt. Pleasant (803) 884-2560

Variety Store...144
Municipal Yacht Basin, 17 Lockwood Drive (803) 723-6325

Village Cafe...146
415 Mill Street, Mt. Pleasant , S.C. (803) 884-8095

Alexander's Station has arrived bringing back memories of romantic old train stations and great Lowcountry fare as well as the tradition of "going up to Summerville!" Harvey Poole and his talented partners can take a bow. They brought a twentieth century style royalty to Charleston with their much acclaimed restaurant, Eighty Two Queen. Now they've ventured to the once sleepy town of Summerville to throw a feast for the eager and hungry townfolk.

Away from Charleston, twenty-two miles westerly, along the line the Southern Railway travels, lies Summerville. Nestled in a pine forest, the town runs along a ridge extending from the Cooper River to the Ashley River. Charlestonians long thought Summerville to be a healthful place to go as it was away from the east winds and the heat. When "unpleasantness" hit Charleston, people fled to Summerville. "The height, in contrast to the low country, bestows warm days, but a delightful coolness that fills the air at night making for a comfortable sleep," so exalted a journal of 1879.

Lunch offers starters, light bites, soups, and salads including the Lowcountry Shrimp Salad, Fried Chicken Salad, and Seafood Pasta. Lowcountry lunches (that's a mid-day dinner) feature a Pork Loin with Rosemary and Garlic, Barbequed Shrimp with Grits and Daufuskie Deviled Crabs. In short, all things you'd expect at supper, but that's Southern style to you Northerners! At dinner, (by Yankee definition, at night) they are available again as well as traditional Crabcakes, Oysters Alexander, Beaufort Stew, plus steaks, pastas and today's catch. The recipes are marvelous just like each dish that comes to the table! Here's a tip: you can't go wrong!

14

As for the recipes, the Black Bean Soup is something you'll whip up repeatedly. The Shrimp and Cucumber Salad is a great make ahead dish for a warm day and Collard Greens are making a comeback! The Seafood Quiche is great for entertaining. For the sweet tooth nothing beats that favorite memory of an American childhood, Toll House Pie!

Beaufort stew is a Carolina classic made of chicken, shrimp, Hillshire sausage and vegetables in a tomato broth and served over white rice. Beaufort Stew is a recipe that originated in Beaufort, South Carolina, so Beaufort folks say, but just a stone's throw away the town of Frogmore lays claim to this dish in a squaring off rivalry that is uncompromising. Alexander's defers to Beaufort (it's bigger than Frogmore). But if it is indeed the heritage and legacy of local Frogmorians, we need to have a twitch of conscious here. We could start a grass roots movement and ask for Frogmore Stew!

Summerville is home to internationally known Southern genre artist Samuel Ravenal Gaillard whose art gallery is settled in among a host of wonderful shops. Look at the art credits for this book and you will see representations of his Lowcountry art. Sweet, gentle, hospitable Summerville is the essence of what Southern means. Alexander's Station is another reason to discover the charms of this Southern town and get acquainted with some pretty wonderful people.

Shrimp and Cucumber Salad

1 lb. medium shrimp,
  peeled, boiled, drained
  and cooled
1 medium onion, diced
1 bell pepper, diced
1/2 cup celery, diced
2 cucumbers, peeled,
  seeded and diced

1 cup mayonnaise
2 Tbsp. fresh dill
  chopped
2 Tbsp. lemon juice
2 dashes Tabasco
  sauce
Salt and freshly
  ground pepper

Combine all ingredients in large mixing bowl. Adjust salt and pepper to your taste.
Serves 4-6

BBQ Shrimp
in Southern Comfort Sauce

1/4 lb. bacon, diced
1/2 cup red onion, diced
1/2 cup red bell pepper
1/2 cup green bell pepper
1 (1.7 oz.) bottle
  Southern Comfort

2 (14 oz.) bottles of
  Heinz ketchup
1/2 cup brown sugar
Salt & pepper to taste
1 Tbsp. butter
2 lbs. shrimp, peeled

Cook bacon until 3/4 done. Add onion and peppers; sauté until done. Flame with Southern Comfort. Add ketchup, brown sugar plus salt and pepper to taste. Simmer for 10 minutes, then cool. Will last under refrigeration for several weeks.

Sauté or poach shrimp in 1 tablespoon of butter. Place in Southern Comfort BBQ Sauce and simmer for 1 minute. Serve over grits topped with cheddar cheese and garnish with chopped scallions.
Serves 6

16

Black Bean Soup

2 lb. black beans	1 small carrot, diced fine
1 gallon water	2 tsp. salt
1/2 lb. smoked sausage, chopped	1 tsp. black pepper
1 small onion, diced fine	1 tsp. chili powder
1 tsp. garlic, diced fine	1/2 tsp. cumin
4 pieces celery, diced fine	4 dashes of Tabasco sauce

Thoroughly wash beans and soak overnight in cold water. Drain the beans the next day and add remaining ingredients. Bring to a boil. Boil for 1/2 hour, then reduce heat to medium. Cover and let cook for 2 hours stirring frequently.

Garnish with shredded cheddar cheese, diced red onion, sour cream, and a slice of jalapeno pepper.

Yield: 1 1/2 gallons

Seafood Quiche

1 (9 inch) pie shell	1 cup milk
1/4 lb. scallops	1 cup cheddar cheese, shredded
1/4 lb. shrimp, peeled and deveined	1/4 cup sherry wine
1/4 lb. crabmeat (special white)	Salt and freshly ground pepper
6 eggs	4 Tbsp. fresh parsley, chopped

Preheat oven to 375°.

Arrange raw seafood in pie shell. Mix eggs, milk, sherry, salt and pepper. Pour over seafood already in pie shell. Top with shredded cheddar cheese and bake for 1 hour. Let cool 15 minutes before slicing. Top with chopped parsley and serve.

Yield: 4 large portions

Beaufort Stew

1 cup celery,
  diced large
1/2 cup onion,
  diced large
1 cup mixed sweet peppers
  (red, yellow, green) diced
1/2 cup kernel corn
1/4 cup cooking oil

1 lb. shrimp (30 pieces)
  peeled
2 lb. chicken breast,
  boneless,
  skinless and grilled
1 lb. andoulli hot
  sausage, sliced
6 cups white rice,
  cooked

Tomato Stock

3 cups V-8 juice
2 bay leaves
2 Tbsp. brown sugar
1 tsp. thyme

2 tsp. cornstarch (mixed
  with 2 tsp. water)
Salt and black pepper to
  taste

Sauté vegetables in large heavy skillet, using 1/4 cup oil, until vegetables are half cooked. Add remaining ingredients except rice and sauté for 5 minutes. Add tomato stock ingredients and simmer for 10 minutes. Thicken with cornstarch. Serve over white rice.

Yield: 6 portions

Lowcountry Collard Greens

12 slices bacon
1 sweet onion, julienned
1 bunch collard greens,
  washed thoroughly

2 Tbsp. Tabasco sauce
2 oz. vinegar
1/3 cup sugar
1 tsp. black pepper
Salt to taste

Dice bacon and brown in pot. Add julienned onion and sauté until tender. Add greens and cover with water. Add remaining ingredients and simmer until tender. Adjust seasoning. Yield: 12 portions

Toll House Pie

2 eggs
1/2 cup flour, unsifted
1/2 cup sugar
1/2 cup brown sugar, packed
1 cup butter, melted and
   returned to room temp.

1 cup chopped walnuts
1 cup (6 oz. pkg.)
   semi-sweet real
   chocolate morsels
1 (9 in.) pie shell,
   unbaked

Preheat oven to 325°.

In a large bowl, beat eggs until foamy; beat in flour, sugar and brown sugar until well blended. Blend in melted butter, walnuts and Nestle morsels. Pour into pie shell and bake for 1 hour. Remove from oven. Serve warm with whipped cream or ice cream. Garnish with whole walnuts if desired.

Yield: 1 pie

Lemon Chess Pie

1/2 cup sugar
4 tsp. cornstarch
2 tsp. lemon zest
4 eggs, room
   temperature

1/3 cup lemon juice
5 Tbsp. butter, melted
   and cooled
1 partially baked 9" pie
   shell

Preheat oven to 325°.

Combine sugar and cornstarch in a large bowl and mix pressing out any lumps. Stir in lemon zest. Beat in eggs, one at a time. Stir in lemon juice. Blend in butter. Pour filling into pie shell and bake until puffed and golden brown 50-60 minutes. Cool before serving. (Filling will thicken and fall somewhat and acquire jelly-like texture as it cools.)

Yield: 1 pie

A.W. SHUCK'S
OYSTER BAR

RAKING FOR OYSTERS.

Just around the corner from the famous Public Market, A.W. Shuck's is Charleston's robust oyster bar. This "in" place is forever crowded with garrulous diners. Serving from 11:00 A.M. to midnight, Shuck's is charged with an air of conviviality. Once a Nabisco warehouse, the oyster bar is made of floor joists from the old building. The fun is to sit at the oyster bar, order one or two of this and two or three of that and watch the shuckers shuck!

The menu is simple, but everything is fresh and delicious. The big items are Oysters and Clams on the Half Shell. A rich pipin' hot Seafood Chowder, Shrimp Creole, Deviled Crab, Shrimp Fried Rice and varied daily specials round out the menu. Shucks is a come anytime, stand up, sit down happening, a haven for the weary of foot, and dedicated to seeing that Charleston eats oysters! Oyster roasts are a favorite pastime along the Carolina Coast in those well-known cooler months with an "r" in them. Some say it's a myth about the "r" months dating to the days before modern refrigeration. Although oysters are prepared a number of ways in Charleston: broiled, fried, stewed, plus dozens of others, none surpasses Shuck's Special. Topped with crab, Parmesan and bacon, it becomes a tantalizing combination of flavors. They're marvelous as an hors d' oeuvre, for a buffet, or triple the number for a fulfilling entree!

Shuck's Special

Fresh oysters or clams	Bread crumbs
White crabmeat	Parmesan cheese
Butter	Bacon

Shuck 1 fresh oyster or clam and loosen from bottom shell. Cover with crabmeat and dot with butter. Sprinkle on bread crumbs and Parmesan cheese and top with 1/4 strip of bacon. Broil until brown and serve immediately.

Geeche Bowl Dinner for 4

1/2 lb. smoked sausage
1/2 lb. chicken tenders
1/2 lb. shrimp, peeled
  and deveined
1 15 oz. can red kidney
  beans with juice
1 Tbsp. garlic, chopped
2 cups mixed vegetables
(carrots, broccoli,
  mushrooms,
  squash) chopped
1 cup sugar snap
  peas
2 Tbsp. blackening
  spice
4 cups rice, cooked

In a heavy skillet, sauté sausage, chicken, and shrimp. Add kidney beans with juice, vegetables and spices. Simmer for 15 minutes or until vegetables are tender. Serve over rice.
   Serves 4

Ellis Creek Casserole for One

1 oz. mushrooms, sliced
1 oz. green onions, sliced
6 oz. red snapper filet
1 Tbsp. butter
Pinch salt & pepper
2 oz. pepper jack
  cheese, shredded
2 Tbsp. walnuts,
  chopped

Preheat oven to 375°.
   Place mushrooms and green onions in bottom of small casserole dish. Place fish over vegetables and top with butter and seasonings. Bake for 20 minutes. Add cheese and walnuts, then continue baking until cheese melts.
   Serves 1

Shrimp Newberg

1/4 lb. butter	1/2 cup sherry
1 cup flour	1 tsp. lemon
1 quart milk	juice
1 1/2 lbs. shrimp	1 tsp. paprika
cooked, peeled,	3 egg yolks
and deveined	8 cups rice, cooked

Melt butter in top of double boiler, add flour and cook 10 minutes, stirring constantly. Add milk and continue to stir until sauce boils. Add cooked shrimp, sherry, lemon juice and paprika. Slowly stir in egg yolks, reduce heat and simmer 10 minutes longer. Serve over hot rice.
Serves 6-8

Shrimp Fried Rice

1 pint whole grain rice	1 large onion,
2 1/2 tsp. salt	chopped
1 lb. shrimp,	2 eggs, beaten
cooked, peeled,	1 1/2 tsp. soy sauce
and deveined	1 cup bean sprouts
1/4 cup cooking oil	Salt and pepper

Bring 6 1/2 quarts of water to a boil, add 1 pint of rice and 2 1/2 teaspoons salt. Cook rice until tender, stirring occasionally. When rice is cooked, pour into a colander to drain.

Cut shrimp lengthwise and set aside. Heat oil in a heavy skillet. Stir in shrimp and onion. Beat eggs and add to pan, stir and cook 2 1/2 minutes. Stir in rice and continue to cook another 3 minutes. Sprinkle soy sauce overall and mix well. Add the bean sprouts and cook 3 minutes longer. Season with salt and pepper.
Serves 6-8

BARBADOES

THE MILLS HOUSE

Just a short distance from the Market on historic Meeting Street stands a small luxury hotel of exquisite charm. The Mills House Hotel is a faithful reconstruction of the 1853 original. Now, as then, it reflects the luster of Charleston's social life in its gleaming appointments. In agreement with preservationists, the old building was dismantled. The original terra cotta pediments were discovered and copied in long lasting fiberglass. The iron balcony made by the finest Philadelphia ironworks was saved and additional copies were made for the Queen Street side of the building.

From the moment you enter the hotel's gas-lighted portals you have the feeling something special awaits you. Sparkling chandeliers abound. One outstanding crystal creation is from the Belle Meade Mansion in Nashville. Priceless furniture fills the public rooms and leads to one of the most romantic dining rooms in the South. The Barbadoes Room at any time of day is elegant. An unending array of magnificent arches fills the room and is repeated in a mirrored wall for sheer drama. Plantation fans gently whir above the chairs of mocha velvet. Tables draped in crisp white linen are all set with sparkling stem ware and fresh flowers.

The cuisine lives up to the setting with Lowcountry food the speciality. Many dishes have a West Indies flavor in keeping with Charleston's ties to the Caribbean, extending back to the seventeenth century. Many early Charlestonians were Englishmen who first settled plantations in the West Indies. When they later moved up to South Carolina, they brought Barbadian touches that influenced not just their architecture, but their whole way of life. You will find this tantalizing taste discovery in the Barbadoes Room.

Serving both lunch and dinner, the staff has one of the best career waiters you could find. Reggie Simmons served Prince Charles and Lady Di when they were in Charleston. He demonstrates the professional qualities of graciousness and efficiency associated with the finest European tradition.

Outstanding entrees such as the Pork Tenderloin served with a curried fruit compote are raved about. Chicken West Indies is served in a coconut shell fragrant with curry, pineapple and chutney. The Coquilles St. Jacques is delicious and festive. For dessert, the Chocolate Mousse is a favorite. Prepare it at home and your reputation will be guaranteed.

Located in the heart of this beautiful and historic city, you can walk everywhere! The Mills House gives you a chance to experience fine food and warm hospitality. The grandeur of the grand old hotel has been preserved. To stay here is a delight! General Robert E. Lee was a guest when he stayed in Charleston in 1861 and even Mark Twain enjoyed a chat in the lobby while lighting up a cigar! Why not indulge yourself in the very personal luxuries the Mills House offers, lean back and sigh with the contentment of another era!

Coquilles St. Jacques

1 1/2 lbs. scallops
1 Tbsp. shallots, chopped
1/4 Tsp. salt
Dash of pepper
1/2 cup dry white wine

1 cup cream
1 Tbsp. flour
4 Tbsp. butter, softened
Parmesan cheese, grated

In a saucepan combine the scallops, shallots, salt, pepper and wine. Bring to a boil and simmer for 2 minutes. Remove the scallops and divide them into 4 scallop shells or small individual baking dishes. Over a high heat cook the remaining liquid until reduced to half. Then add cream and boil until sauce has become as thick as syrup. Combine the butter and flour. Lower the heat on the sauce and slowly stir in the butter little by little. Pour the sauce over the scallops, sprinkle with Parmesan cheese and brown under the broiler. Yield: 4 portions

West Indies Chicken

1 serving of precooked chicken cut into cubes	1 serving of cooked rice
1 Tbsp. butter	1 tsp. shredded coconut
3 oz. curry sauce	1/2 banana
1 coconut cut in half	1/4 fresh pineapple

Sauté chicken in butter until brown. Drain, add chicken to curry sauce, bring to a boil. Put heated rice into coconut shell. Pour chicken curry over it. Sprinkle with shredded coconut. Cut banana lengthwise and place around side of coconut shell. Garnish plate with fresh pineapple or other seasonal fruit.

Chutney can be served on the side.

Yield: one portion

Curry Sauce:

3 Tbsp. butter	1 Tbsp. curry powder
2 medium onions, minced	2 c. chicken stock
1 tart apple, chopped	1/2 cup cream
1 clove garlic, unpeeled	1/4 tsp. salt
1 Tbsp. flour	Freshly ground white pepper

Melt the butter in a large skillet over medium heat and sauté the onions, apple and clove of garlic for 3 to 4 minutes. Remove the garlic. Add the flour and curry and mix. Gradually add the chicken stock while stirring constantly. Cook over a low heat for 25 minutes and stir occasionally. Stir in the cream and salt. Season with pepper to taste. Pour the sauce over the chicken and serve.

Hot Spinach Salad

1 lb. fresh spinach	1/3 cup tarragon
5 strips of bacon	vinegar
2 tsp. olive oil	1/2 tsp. sugar
1/2 tsp. Worcestershire	Juice of 1/2 lemon
1/2 tsp. salt	1 cup hard cooked
1/2 tsp. black pepper	egg, chopped
1/2 tsp. dry mustard	1 cup blue cheese

After washing and drying the spinach, put it in a wooden salad bowl and place in a warm oven, along with the serving plates. Cook the bacon until crisp and set aside. Pour off most of the bacon grease, add the olive oil and heat. Add the Worcestershire sauce, salt, pepper, dry mustard, tarragon vinegar, sugar and lemon juice stirring until thoroughly heated. Remove from heat. Add the chopped egg and blue cheese and mix. Pour hot mixture over the warm spinach and toss. Crumble the bacon and sprinkle over the salad. Serve immediately on warm plates.

Serves 4

Chicken Salad in a Coconut

4 oz. boneless	Pinch of salt
chicken breast,	Lime juice to taste
precooked and diced	4 pineapple chunks
1 stalk celery, diced	4 pecans, shelled
Mayonnaise to taste	Grated coconut
Curry powder to taste	

Cut a fresh coconut in half. Mix chicken, celery, mayonnaise, curry powder, salt and lime juice together. Place chicken salad in shell. Garnish with pineapple, pecans and grated coconut. Serves one

Chocolate Mousse

1/2 lb. dark sweet chocolate cut into small pieces	5 eggs, separated
	1/2 cup heavy cream
6 Tbsp. water	1 tsp. vanilla extract
Pinch of salt	
3 Tbsp. light rum	1 Tbsp. sugar

Melt the chocolate pieces, along with 6 tablespoons of water and a pinch of salt in the top of a double boiler. Stir occasionally until chocolate is dissolved and smooth. Pour the chocolate into a mixing bowl and add the rum and stir.

After separating the eggs, add the yolks to the chocolate and mix well. In a separate bowl, beat the egg whites with an electric mixer until soft peaks are formed. Add the chocolate mixture to the egg whites and mix with a wire whisk. Pour the mixture into small cups and refrigerate overnight.

Whip the heavy cream until thick, then add vanilla and sugar and continue whipping until stiff. Place a spoonful of whipped cream on top of each chilled chocolate mousse and serve.

Serves 6-8

Beaumont's

The newest and freshest version of French hospitality and ambiance in a city known for both is Beaumont's. Owner Jean-Marc Petin has a reputation with Charlestonians for his work here. While on a sabbatical in France, he received the Award of Paris for his talents. With a piano in the entry, wafting melodies right out into the street, you can't help but take a glimpse into Beaumont's. Just pick up the rhythm of a Cole Porter tune and dance right in! It is an invitation to step into a rich, exciting ambiance that is very French, being both informal and elegant.

Simple brick walls and exceptionally tall ceilings, beautiful iron gates and gleaming wooden floors are architectural features. Leaded glass and polished brass appointments add sparkle to what was once the stable of a large East Bay mansion that fronted on the Cooper river. Family portraits are mounted over the bar and many tables overlook a green courtyard. But don't fear it's too formal; Jean-Marc is quick to inform you they are *not* stuffy, *not* overpriced. They just want to be thought of as a nice neighborhood restaurant.

The emphasis is on the quality of food. Chef Christian Deslandes prepares traditional classic entrees of salmon, sweetbreads, rabbit, duckling, liver foi gras, and pâtés. Innovative recipes such as the Chicken Breast with Tarragon Sauce is sublime as well as the St. Jacques Grilles Aux Asparagus. Both are great company fare. The Potato Stuffed with Escargot is a superb appetizer as well

30

as a surprising party dish. The wine list is very complete and priced between $12 and $90 a bottle. The Petin family started a kind of a revolution in town because they add only a few dollars to the price of each bottle.

The pastry chef Tony DaSilva delivers a heavenly Supreme Au Chocolat. My favorite is the Creme Brûlée. This is the voguish dessert made famous by *Le Cirque* in New York. Hands down, Beaumont's desserts are better than the QE2! Bringing a taste of Provence to historic Charleston, these frugal French are proud their dinner check runs between $10 and $20.with lunch being much less!

St. Jacques Grilles Aux Asparagus

24 asparagus spears	1 large tomato,
Salt and pepper to taste	peeled and diced
1 cup heavy cream	6 cups white rice,
24 scallops	cooked

Cut the asparagus spears in half. Cook the ends **only** in a pan of water, seasoned with salt and pepper, for 30 minutes. Put cooked asparagus ends into a food processor along with the heavy cream and blend. Pour cream and asparagus sauce into a pan and reduce for a few minutes.

Cook tips of asparagus for 15 minutes and keep warm. Brush some oil on the scallops and add salt and freshly ground pepper to taste. Grill the scallops for 3 minutes on each side.

Place a serving of rice in a mound in the center of each plate. Pour the sauce around the rice. Then place around the plate, on top of the sauce, a scallop, an asparagus tip, tomato, a scallop, an asparagus tip, tomato, etc. until the circle is complete.

Yield: 6 appetizer size portions

Mediterranean Vegetable soup

2 Tbsp. sweet butter
1 small onion, minced
1 leek, white part only,
   split, carefully
   washed and minced
2 quarts of water
2 medium-sized potatoes,
   peeled and cut into cubes
5 cloves of garlic, minced
1 bouquet garni made of:
   1 sprig thyme, 1 bay leaf,
   1 sprig parsley, 1 sprig
   basil, bound together
   with a cotton string
2 small zucchini, peeled
   and cut into cubes

2 cups cooked or canned
   navy or great
   northern beans
2 cups green beans, diced
1 medium tomato, peeled,
   seeded and diced
1/3 cup spaghetti, broken
   into small pieces
Salt and pepper to taste

Pistou

3 cloves garlic, crushed
12 leaves basil, chopped
6 Tbsp. Parmesan
   cheese, grated
3 Tbsp. olive oil

Melt the butter in a soup kettle over low heat. Sauté the onion and leek until almost melted. Add the 2 quarts of water, potatoes, garlic, bouquet garni and bring to a boil. Reduce the heat and simmer for 45 minutes.

Add the zucchini, navy beans, green beans, tomato, and spaghetti to the pot and boil slowly for 15 minutes. Season with salt and freshly ground pepper to taste.

While the soup is cooking, prepare the *pistou*. Place the garlic, basil leaves and Parmesan cheese in a soup tureen and blend to a paste with a wooden spoon; then drop by drop beat in the olive oil. When the soup is ready remove the bouquet garni and sir one cup of soup gradually into the *pistou*. Pour the remainder of the soup into the tureen and serve with hot French bread.

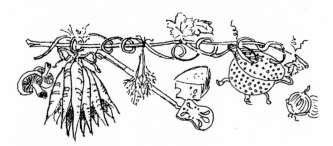

Sautéed Chicken Breast
with Tarragon Sauce

2 boneless chicken breasts
Flour for dusting chicken
1 bouquet fresh tarragon
3/4 cup heavy cream
1 cup white wine

1 cup chicken broth
3 Tbsp. butter
Salt and pepper to taste
2 cups white rice, cooked

Flour the chicken breasts. Melt the butter in a large pan and brown the chicken breasts on each side. Finely chop the tarragon and put it on top of the chicken breasts. Add the wine and the chicken broth and let reduce for a few minutes. Add the heavy cream and let reduce again. Place rice on serving plate with chicken on top and pour sauce over chicken.
Serves 2

Crème Brûlée

6 egg yolks	The rind of 1/3 lemon
3/4 cup 4 X sugar	The rind of 1/2 orange
2 1/4 cups heavy cream	

Preheat oven to 275°.

In a mixing bowl, beat the egg yolks and sugar until mixture is pale yellow and thick. In a small saucepan, bring the cream to a boil. While beating the egg yolks let the hot cream trickle into them and mix well.

Pour the mixture into a double boiler and add the lemon and orange rind. Cook over medium heat, while stirring constantly, until custard thickens . **Do not let it boil!**

Pour through a strainer into a buttered shallow baking dish, thereby removing the lemon and orange rind. Bake in a very slow oven for 1 1/4 hours or until the custard is set. Remove from oven and cool. Refrigerate overnight.

Yield: 8 portions

Bed and breakfast are the tradition of Charleston's smaller, more personal inns such as the Vendue.

39 Church Street.   Robert Siller

Supreme au Chocolat

8 oz. chocolate chips	1 cup expresso coffee
2 oz. bitter chocolate	1 cup creme patissiere
1/2 lb. butter	(recipe follows)
5 egg yolks	1 pkg. lady fingers

Melt both chocolates and the butter in a double boiler. Add the expresso and the creme patissiere and stir. Remove from heat.

Stir in the egg yolks. Place bowl into a larger bowl of ice and whip chocolate mixture for 15 minutes.

Grease a pan. Cover bottom and sides of pan with lady fingers. Pour chocolate mixture into the pan and refrigerate for 24 hours.

Creme Patissiere:

1 cup milk	2 egg yolks
1 tsp. vanilla	3 egg whites
3 Tbsp. of flour	2 Tbsp. sugar

Bring the milk, sugar and vanilla to a boil. Reduce the heat and stir in the flour and the eggs and cook for 2 minutes.

Bessinger's Bar-B-Que & Buffeteria

Barbecue is pure Americana! It is a part of a Southern heritage that has traveled across the country. Bessinger's Bar-B-que & Buffeteria, out on the Savannah Highway, provides a change of pace and is a real family pleaser. The secret to great barbecue is the sauce. Father Joe Sr. created it over 35 years ago and since then it has been talked about, envied, and copied, but never duplicated.

Here at what the owners term "Buffeteria" you'll will find black eyed peas, fragrant greens, fried chicken, and tender chunks of unrivaled barbecued pork and beef ribs. The eatery also features the freshest salad fixin's, great cole slaw, true Southern corn bread, and peach cobbler. Be sure to try the sweet potato soufflé! Not at all like that nervous puff, the classic soufflé, the sweet potato variety is firm, but light and delicious. Just add a sprinkling of raisins and coconut and, *voila*, you have a delightful vegetable or a surprising dessert. I serve it at Thanksgiving and other company meals and everyone loves it! This dish has its origins in the South. You'll never find it on a yankee menu!

Great sandwiches for a beach picnic can be picked up here 7 days a week. The Buffeteria, however, is only open Thursday thru Saturday evenings from 5:00 to 8:00 P.M. and on Sunday from 12:00 noon to 8:00 P.M. You'll come, ya hear!

Sweet Potato Soufflé

6 medium sweet potatoes	1/2 cup light brown
3 Tbsp. butter	sugar
2 eggs, beaten	1/4 cup raisins
1/4 cup sugar	1/4 cup coconut
1/2 tsp. salt	Cinnamon

Preheat oven to 350°.

Cook, peel and mash the sweet potatoes. Add butter and eggs to potatoes and beat until light and fluffy. Add all the remaining ingredients, reserving a little coconut. Place in a buttered 2 quart casserole, and sprinkle with cinnamon. Bake for about 30 minutes. A few minutes before removing from oven sprinkle with remaining coconut and brown. Serves 6

Southern Corn Bread

1 3/4 cups yellow corn meal (plain)	1 tsp. salt
	2 Tbsp. sugar
3/4 cup self rising flour	2 eggs
2 1/2 tsp. double acting baking powder	2 Tbsp. melted shortening
	1 cup milk

Preheat oven to 400°.

Grease pie tin or iron skillet and heat in oven. Sift dry ingredients into a large bowl. Add eggs, melted shortening and milk all at once. Stir only until all ingredients are wet. Pour batter into heated tin or skillet. Bake for 25 to 30 minutes or until golden brown.

Serves 4-6

Cole Slaw

1 medium head of cabbage, grated	2 carrots, grated
	1/4 cup mayonnaise
1/2 cup sweet pickles, chopped	2 Tbsp. sugar
	1/4 tsp. salt

Mix all ingredients and serve well chilled.
Serves 6-8

Peach Cobbler

1/2 Tbsp. cornstarch
1/4 tsp. ground nutmeg
1/4 tsp. ground cinnamon
1/2 cup brown sugar

1/2 cup water
4 cups sliced peaches
1 Tbsp. lemon juice
1 Tbsp. butter

Preheat oven to 400°.

Combine cornstarch, nutmeg, cinnamon, sugar and water in a saucepan. Cook and stir over medium heat until thickened. Add peaches, lemon juice and butter. Cook until peaches are heated through. Pour peach mixture into 8 inch round baking dish. Top with strips of pastry. Bake for 20 to 25 minutes until the strips of pastry turn brown.

Serves 6-8

Pastry Crust

1 1/2 cups all-purpose flour
1/2 tsp. salt

1/2 cup shortening
4-5 Tbsp. cold water

Sift the flour and salt together. Work in the shortening with a pastry blender or knife until pieces are the size of small peas. Add ice water gradually and form into a ball. Roll out on lightly floured surface until about 1/8 inch thick. You will have enough pastry to make a lattice top. Cut strips of pastry 1/2 to 3/4 inch wide. Lay strips on top of peach mixture at 1-inch intervals. Fold back alternate strips as you weave cross-strips over and under.

Yield: double crust for 8-inch pie.

Bocci's

Walking along Church Street, just before the Public Market, you can amble into the inviting atmosphere of a "Little Italy." Don't expect the commonplace Americanized Italian here! The overall experience is like a trip to the trattorias of Northern Italy. Tuscany was the birthplace of those divine creators Michelangelo and de Vinci. Now, to all divine things Italian, add Bocci.

Fragrant aromas and the friendliest of people invite you for a delicious lunch or dinner. Colin and David are the soul of hospitality! Settle comfortably into one of the cozy terra cotta colored dining rooms. Savor the feeling of Florence or Trentino or Bologna with hand painted murals of vineyards creating a bucolic serenity. Choose a wine and capture a mellow moment.

Sauces are all freshly made and served with a much lighter hand. Bocci's doesn't stop at making their own fresh fettucine and angel hair pastas, they even hand pull their own mozzarella! Heavenly béchamel sauces are made from scratch to accompany the Lemon-Basil Chicken and the Shrimp Alfredo dishes.

The pesto recipe has many uses. This is a Genoese sauce of fresh basil, olive oil, garlic, cheese and pine nuts making it excellent when served with basic pasta dishes. It is also great for accent over braised chicken or to flavor soups, stews or salad dressings. My newlywed daughter Tia, makes extra pesto and pours it into an ice cube tray to freeze. She then empties the cubes into a ziplock bag to defrost when needed. Its yummy with just a good bread!

Thanks Bocci for dishes that bring such contentment!

Béchamel (Basic White Sauce)

5 cups whole milk	1 bay leaf
1 small yellow onion	1 tsp. salt
peeled & quartered	1/4 tsp. white
	pepper

Pour milk into sauce pan along with onion, bay leaf, salt and white pepper. Heat to a slow boil, stirring often.

Roux:

2 Tbsp. butter   3 Tbsp. flour

In another saucepan melt the butter over low heat. Blend in the flour and cook slowly, stirring, until the butter and flour froth together for 2 minutes. (Do not let roux turn brown.) Remove roux from heat. When the roux stops bubbling, pour it into the hot milk all at one time. Beat vigourously with a wire whip to blend the two together. Strain.

Shrimp Alfredo

2 oz. white wine	2 oz. Parmesan
4 oz. half & half	cheese, grated
4 oz. béchemel sauce	Salt & pepper
1 oz. fresh basil, chopped	6 oz. fettucine pasta
15-20 medium shrimp	cooked al denté
peeled & deveined	

Heat wine, half & half and béchamel to a simmer. Add basil and shrimp and return to a simmer. Turn over shrimp and add Parmesan cheese. Stir while adding salt and pepper to taste. Simmer 30-45 seconds and toss in pasta.
Serves 2-4

Lemon-Basil Chicken

2 chicken breasts,
  boneless & skinless
4 oz. olive oil
6 oz. all purpose flour
4-5 mushrooms, sliced
2 cloves garlic, minced
2-3 scallions, sliced
2 oz. dry white wine

1 oz. fresh basil,
  chopped
2 lemons, cut in half
6 oz. béchamel sauce
Salt & pepper
8 oz. angel hair
  pasta cooked
  al denté

Slice each chicken breast into 8-10 slices. Heat oil in large frying pan. Dredge chicken slices in flour and brown in hot oil for 3-4 minutes. Add mushrooms & garlic. Stir and cook about 30 seconds. Add scallions, white wine, basil and juice of both lemons. Add béchamel, and salt and pepper to taste. Stir in cooked pasta. Serves 2-4

Angel Hair Pasta with Shrimp & Spicy Pesto

1/4 cup olive oil
50-60 medium shrimp,
  peeled & deveined
1/2 cup pesto*
1/2 cup julienne sundried
  tomatoes reconstituted*

1/2 cup white wine
2 cups heavy cream
Salt & pepper
1 lb. angel hair pasta
  cooked al denté

Heat oil on medium in large skillet. Add shrimp and cook until just beginning to change color, (about 1-2 minutes). Stir in pesto and sundried tomatoes. Deglaze with white wine and add cream. Salt and pepper to taste and simmer 1-2 minutes - until sauce just begins to thicken. Mix pasta into sauce. Serves 6-8

Basil Pesto

3 oz. fresh basil
3 oz. fresh spinach
1/2 cup pine nuts or walnuts
1/2 cup grated Parmesan
2 tbsp. chopped garlic
1/2 cup olive oil
1 Tbsp. black pepper
1 Tbsp. salt

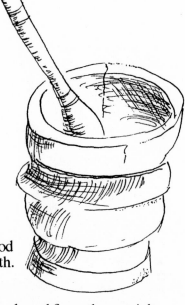

Pour all ingredients into a food processor and blend until smooth.
Yield: 2 cups

*A prepared pesto may be purchased from the specialty foods department at your local grocery. Also sundried tomatoes may be purchased already reconstituted.

Pears in Wine

1 1/2 cups sugar
1/2 cup water
6 pears, peeled with
    stem intact

1 cup sweet red
    wine
1 cinnamon stick
1 piece lemon peel
6 sprigs of mint

Heat the sugar and water until sugar is dissolved. Add the remaining ingredients and simmer for 15 minutes. Remove the pears and return the wine syrup to the boil until it thickens. Pour over the pears and refrigerate. Garnish with mint and serve. Serves 6

Carolina's

Tia Sillero-Purcell

Carolina's is a real Southern surprise. Once a seaman's tavern, it is just steps off the water and the old docks which were the center of activity in this bustling harbor.

The fact that the setting is a seashell tabby building dating from the mid-1700's conjures up a romantic fantasy straight out of a Gothic novel! Enveloped by the fog, our heroine lifts up her long skirts and gathers her hooded cape, as she steps from the quaint charm of the waterfront area at Exchange Street. All teary-eyed, she crosses the cobblestones to meet her paramour who defended her honor in a duel. She opens the door to Carolina's with blue morning glories vining all around.

Un Unh, darlin! *this* Carolina's is a big city bistro bustling with activity. It is the place to see and be seen among the movers and shakers of the city's elite. This Carolina's is Southern, yet citified, old guard and avant-garde; however you describe that Carolina's style, you can be sure it will be full of surprises.

The sidewalk dining area is centered around an open bar, and is accented with stark French bistro posters that line the walls of this trend-setting, sleek environment. An open kitchen reveals a flurry of motion. This is the perfect place for a glass of wine, a small dish, a great salad or a dessert and coffee. Pastas and omelets are served around the clock. The Perdita's Room is the tucked away dining room every Charlestonian books a reservation for well in advance. With rich, marbleized walls and comfortable bankettes, it's sophisticated and more formal.

One look at the menu and you'll be tickled and tempted. Carolina's gave birth to a culinary renaissance. Chris Weihs and Rose Darden started serving grits with shad roe, introducing grits as a grain that could go beyond breakfast. And Gosh, Wow, Zowie, they propelled grits into mainstream cuisine!

Appetizers of Fresh Mussels Steamed in Chardonnay with garlic, plus a luscious Cream of Butternut Bisque with bits of Crabmeat reached out to tempt me. A heavenly salad came to the table of mixed baby greens touched with a smooth Peanut Raspberry Viniagrette with the zing of ginger, herbs and extra virgin olive oil.

The entrees continued an assault on my senses: Grilled Tuna Nicrosse; Fresh Quail stuffed with Collard Greens; Grilled medallians of Beef Tenderloin with Shrimp and Scallops in Sonoma Tomato Butter; The Salmon with Roasted Pepper, Leeks and Shitake Mushrooms in a Lime Viniagrette sounded tantalizing. A dicision was needed. Should I go innovative, iconoclastic, International or head South?

I took a stand. I voted a straight Southern ticket. I started with an appetizer of Blackeyed Peacakes. I ordered the succulent Grouper in Almond Black Seseme crust, just to taste the passion of every Southern soul, Fried Green Tomatoes! A side dish of Carolina Grits, the consistancy of mashed potatoes came to the table; and for dessert Sweet Grits Cake with sauteed Raspberries and Blackberries. A second dinner had to happen. The Sautéed Carolina Crab Cakes with Rémoulade Sauce, lured me back the next night. I enjoyed the taste of the South in my mouth with the BBQ Baby Back ribs, with Carolina's own seductive sauce.

Hands down, this is the first place Rhett would have walked into when he came back into town.

Chris says half of his customers are "locals." I've studied the crowd: South of Broad types, all Brooks Brothered and suspendered sauntering in from their offices; proud noble matriarchs and patriarchs; hip and trendy yuppies, plus bright eyed visitors in from a day of golf or touring. Stop anyone on the street and ask their favorite restaurants and when rolling off their favorites, they'll invariably sing out, Ah.....Car-O-lin-ahs!

Carolina's has everything: great food, style and flair, unsurpassed service, the city's most extensive wine list with over 200 selections, and an elegant ambiance all in this historic setting. (I just spotted a descendent to one of those eight Lords Proprietors!)

All "**Joe Mike**" products including grits, referred to in the following recipes. are available through the mail order department at Carolina's.

Carolina Pea Cakes

1. Pea Mix:

24 oz. black eyed peas	3 large onions, diced
3/4 gal. water	3 tsp. garlic, chopped
1 oz. chicken base	2 jalapenos or 1 tsp.
1 smoked ham hock	**"Joe Mike"** Habanero

Bring all the ingredients to a boil. Lower heat and simmer, stirring frequently. When peas are fully cooked, remove ham hock. Drain broth and reserve for later use as soup base.

2. Seasoning Mix:

1/4 tsp. salt	1 Tbsp. thyme
1/4 tsp. dry mustard	1/2 tsp. basil
1/4 tsp. black pepper	1 Tbsp. oregano
Pinch cumin	

Mix all seasoning ingredients together and add to peas.

3. Herb & vegetable mix:

2 Tbsp. garlic, chopped	2 green onions, chopped
2 Tbsp. bell pepper, chopped	2 Tbsp. red onion, chopped
2 jalapenos, chopped	1 Tbsp. yellow onion, chopped
3 Tbsp. parsley	
2 Tbsp. fresh cilantro	

Place all herb & vegetable ingredients in a food processor and mince, but not too fine. Then sauté in extra virgin olive oil over low heat for 5 minutes and set aside to cool.

4. Final step:

2 egg yolks	Green onions, sliced
1 cup ground corn bread or bread crumbs	Sour cream

With paddle attached to electric mixer (on speed #1) add one egg yolk and mix, then stop mixer so that some whole peas still remain. Add second yolk and stop mixer. Add seasoning and stop mixer. Add sautéed vegetables and stop mixer. Add corn bread and stop mixer. Patty into 3.5 oz. cakes season to taste. If mix is too wet, add more corn bread. Sauté until browned and serve with sliced green onions and sour cream.

Peanut-Raspberry Vinaigrette

1 cup creamy peanut butter, high quality	1/8 tsp. "**Joe Mike**" firey orange Habanero Sauce
1/4 cup fresh lemon juice	2 Tbsp. parsley, chopped
1/4 cup raspberry vinegar	1 Tbsp. fresh chives, chopped
1/2 tsp. soy sauce	
3/4 cup x-virgin olive oil	1 Tbsp. fresh tarragon, chopped
1/4 cup peanut oil	
1/2 cup raspberry coulis (frozen raspberries pureed and strained)	1 Tbsp. salt
	1 1/2 cups bottled water

In a non corrosive mixing bowl, blend all the ingredients together except the oils. Blend the oils with an electric hand mixer or use a whip. Adjust the seasoning and the acidity. Dressing should be mildly acidic.

Yield: 6 cups

Fried Green Tomatoes

2 fresh, green tomatoes	1 egg, beaten
Salt & black pepper	1/4 cup heavy cream,
1 cup flour, seasoned	added to egg
with salt and pepper	2 cups cornmeal

1. Slice the tomatoes into 1/2" thick slices (do not use the ends, save them for salsa). Dip the slices in the seasoned flour, in the egg wash and in the breading. Pat the crumbs lightly into the tomato slices and refrigerate for at least 15 minutes.

2. Heat a black iron skillet with about 2" deep canola oil until temperature reads about 300 degrees and fry the tomatoes until they are golden brown. (Be very careful, that the temperatures does not rise too high and don't spill the oil. It could cause a flash fire!) A fry daddy or an electric skillet is safer. Serve the tomatoes as a vegetable or with some goat cheese as an appetizer or spread some **"Joe Mike"** Dancin' Pepper Jam over the top.

Carolina Grits

2 2/3 cups **"Joe Mike"** grits	1 Tbsp. salt
6 cups milk	1/4 tsp. white pepper
2 cups cream	1/2 stick unsalted butter

Prior to cooking, rinse grits thoroughly. Pour measured amount into a medium bowl and cover with warm water. Stir grits, then pour off water, including the bran which will rise to the top. Repeat until no more bran rises. Pour off as much water as possible, then stir grits into boiling milk. Reduce heat and allow grits to simmer. Cook approximately 20 minutes, uncovered, stirring occasionally. Add cream as necessary while cooking. Store grits in refrigerator or freezer.

Yield: 8 servings

Carolina's Crab Cakes
with Rémoulade Sauce

1/3 cup red & green bell pepper, diced	1 cup mayonnaise
1/4 cup sweet onion, diced	2 tsp. parsley, chopped
1/8 cup clarified butter	1/2 tsp. "**Joe Mike**"
1/2 tsp. dry mustard	firey Habanero Sauce
1/4 tsp. sea salt	or 1/2 tsp. cayenne
1 cup small white bread cubes (no crust)	1/2 tsp. Worchestershire
	1 lb. lump crabmeat
	Salt and pepper to taste

Sauté vegetables in clarified butter until soft, refrigerate until cool. In a bowl, place the mustard, salt, bread cubes, mayonnaise, parsley, Habanero and Worchestershire sauces and stir well. Pick through the crabmeat for any shells before folding it into the mayonnaise mixture with a rubber spatula. Try not to break up the crabmeat lumps. Refrigerate mixture for 30 minutes. If it is too soft add a few more bread cubes and adjust seasoning. Form crabmeat into 3 or 4 ounce patties and sauté 3 to 5 minutes in a small amount of vegetable oil. Serve with Rémoulade Sauce.

Serves 4.

Rémoulade Sauce:

1 bunch shallots	4 Tbsp. hot Creole mustard
1 stalk celery	
1 clove garlic	Salt & pepper
3 Tbsp. parsley, chopped	1/3 cup vinegar
2 Tbsp. paprika	2/3 cup olive oil

Place the shallots, celery, garlic and parsley in a food processor and blend. Add the paprika, mustard, salt and pepper while stirring. Pour in the vinegar and mix thoroughly. Add the olive oil, a small amount at a time. Stir, tightly seal and refrigerate.

Sweet Grits Cake with Sautéed Seasonal Berries or Fruit

1 1/4 cup golden grits	1/2 tsp. Vanilla extract
2 cups milk	(preferably the
2 cups heavy cream	Mexican vanilla)
1/3 cup sugar	

Prior to cooking, rinse grits thoroughly. Pour measured amount into medium bowl and cover with warm water. Stir grits, then pour off the water, including the bran which will rise to the top. Repeat until no more bran rises. Pour off as much water as possible, then stir the grits into the boiling milk and cream mixture, add sugar and vanilla. Reduce the heat and allow to simmer. Cook approximately 20 minutes uncovered, stirring occasionally. Pour grits into a lightly buttered square 2" high pan and refrigerate for about 1 hour. When grits are completely cold, turn pan onto a cutting board and cut equal squares, about 3"x3"x1" thick.

Sugar mixture:

1 cup granulated sugar	1/4 tsp. ginger
1/4 tsp. cinnamon	Unsalted butter
	1 cup stewed fruit, heated

Mix sugar, cinnamon and ginger thoroughly, dip the grit slices in the sugar and coat them well. Add 1 Tbsp. unsalted butter to a hot frying pan. Over medium heat cook the grits cake until golden brown on both sides, and warm in the center (test with knife tip on your lips! Don't burn them!) Place the grits cake on a plate and ladle the hot fruit over one half. Add pecans, heath bar crunch or peach ice cream. Streak the plate with chocolate sauce (use a squeeze ketchup bottle filled with medium thick chocolate sauce), decorate with a sprig of mint. Even Northerners will love this dessert.

Only five minutes from downtown Charleston but worlds away in character is the Charleston Crab House. On Ashley River Road at the Wappoo Cut bridge is this noisy, happening place. Great for a fun loving group, this is a favorite with the "locals." Come dinner time in the Lowcountry, you'll find both the Charleston blue bloods and the blue collars filling the place to capacity!

Boaters take notice, this is a restaurant you can sail to! Drop anchor at the dock to stop for lunch or dinner served seven days a week. This is a great place to watch the sunset on the Stono River and feel the Atlantic breeze coming in.

A favorite and cherished ritual in the lowlands is the crab boil. All around Charleston you'll find people enjoying a crab boil in their kitchens, in their backyards, or for that matter, even on the beach. If you would like to engage in this dining experience you first have to catch a mess of crabs. They must be alive when dropped into the boiling water. In Gullah, the language of the low lands, the saying is that "de crabs have to walk into de pot!" The crabs must be cooked until they turn bright red. Once cooked, the ritual is to spread newspapers onto the table, deliver your crabs, attack, feast and then roll up the remains and toss. It's fast food and top entertainment combined! For that Charleston touch, serve with peppered sherry.

You may short cut many of these steps by heading straight to the Crab House where Steamed Blue Crabs are served with garlic butter and are a dead on favorite. In fact, Crab cakes, Fried Soft Shell Crab, Deviled Crab and Crabmeat Salad are all on the menu. A broad assortment of other seafood specialities are also offered, such as live Maine lobster, Alaskan king crab, shrimp, oysters, a catch of the day, as well as salads and pastas.

The Crab House gives you the opportunity to discover the protected artery that is the famous Intracoastal Waterway connecting the port of Charleston with other coastal ports. It offers sheltered passage to any destination along the coast. Yachting and boating aficionados navigate to the Crab House on their annual migration to and from Florida.

A local "Old Salt" of a crabbing legend, Nick Sarrano used to pull up in his boat and deliver the freshest of catches right before the customers' eyes. Owner John Keener tells some tall tales about Saranos' expertise in knowing where the goshhawks are nesting, what the osprey are up to and how the crabs are running.

Deviled Crab

1/4 cup butter	2 dashes of Tobasco
1/2 cup celery, finely chopped	1/2 tsp. Worchestershire sauce
1/4 cup green pepper, finely chopped	1 tsp. lemon juice
1 small onion, finely chopped	1 1/2 cups bread crumbs
1 lb. fresh crabmeat	2 Tbsp. fresh parsley, chopped
	Salt and pepper

Preheat oven to 400°.

Melt butter in heavy skillet over medium heat. Sauté celery, green peppers and onions until the onions are translucent. Add crab meat, Tobasco, Worcestershire sauce and lemon juice and continue cooking for 1 minute. Remove from heat and stir in the bread crumbs and parsley.

Fill crab shells or bake in a casserole for 30 minutes or until golden brown.

Serves 6-8

She

Fried Soft-Shell Crabs

6 soft-shell crabs
Salt & fresh pepper
1 egg, slightly beaten

1 cup fine dry bread
  crumbs
Deep fat for frying

Soft-shell crabs should be alive when purchased. Wash carefully to remove sand; place face down on a board. Lift the shell on each side and remove the soft spongy substance underneath. Then turn crab face up: cut off tail and scrape off spongy portions underneath. Wash again and dry on paper towels. Sprinkle with salt and pepper; dip in egg and roll in bread crumbs. Fry in hot deep fat for 3-4 minutes or until golden brown. Drain on unglazed paper and serve. Use your choice of sauce.

Shrimp Salad

1 lb. shrimp, precooked,
  shelled, deveined and
  chopped
1 cup celery, chopped

2 hard boiled eggs,
  chopped fine
1/2 cup mayonnaise
Salt and pepper

Mix all of the above ingredients thoroughly. Season with salt and freshly ground pepper to taste. Serve on lettuce leaves or stuffed into hollowed out tomatoes.
Serves 4

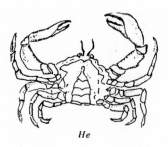

He

In the heart of Charleston's historic district, the East Bay Trading Company stands with pride at the corner of East Bay and Queen. Just around the block from the Dock Street Theater, St. Philip's Church and the Market Place, is this landmark turned restaurant. Built in 1880, this handsome building was once a rice, cotton and tobacco warehouse ideally located close to the busy river front. Ships laden with rich curries from India, molasses from Barbados, and spices from the West Indies sailed into the port daily. The waterfront teemed with life as the products of the fertile lowcountry passed through storehouses just like this one bound for foreign ports.

The structure is an excellent example of Queen Anne style architecture. A series of arched windows, all handsomely etched, line each level of the Bay Street side. The exterior of the building remains exactly as it was a century ago. The aim of the renovation was to retain the architectural heritage of the old warehouse and let it dominate the restaurant. The owners have won recognition for the outstanding results.

This is a place charged with an air of excitement and conviviality. The first floor is rather like a terminal and is a great place for sharing a drink, indulging at the "Oyster, Clam and Other Delectables" bar or having a cup of cappucino aboard the cable car turned rendezvous. An old time Red Rider elevator glides through the 54 foot atrium filled with lush greenery. The upper levels, where more formal dining is the focus, are brightened by an enormous skylight overhead and a wide expanse of windows that look out over the Cooper River. With kitchens on two floors, dinners are served piping hot. A great place to meet for a snack, lunch or dinner, you can order Chicken Jambalaya, Brochette of Scallops, a fabulous Casserole of Drunken Fishes as well as steaks, chops and pastas.

Officially listed in the Historic Register, it's both fun and elegant. The East Bay Trading Company captures the flavor of a bygone era but greets guests with an exciting contemporary air that is very much today.

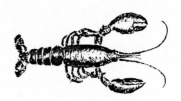

Casserole of Drunken Fishes

Fresh butter
1 clove garlic, minced
1 lobster tail, cut up
1 lb. flounder
8 shrimp, peeled & deveined
8 clams in shell, well drained (but reserve juice)

1/2 lb. scallops
2 Tbsp. bourbon
1/2 lb. red snapper
1-14.5 oz. can stewed tomatoes
Chopped fresh parsley
Fresh pepper
Lemon wedges

Preheat oven to 375°.

Place a cast iron skillet over medium heat on stove. Add 2 tablespoons of butter and minced garlic. Sauté for about 3 minutes. Add lobster, flounder, shrimp, clams and scallops. Mix and continue cooking for 5 minutes. Add the bourbon and reduce. Add red snapper, tomatoes, reserved clam juice, chopped parsley and several grinds of fresh black pepper and bring to a boil. Bake in oven for 15 to 20 minutes. Remove from oven and stir in 1/4 cup of fresh butter. Garnish with lemon wedges and serve.

Yield: 8 portions

Zucchini E.B.T.C.

One medium zucchini,
    thinly sliced
1/4 stick butter
Salt & pepper
Granulated garlic

Pinch of basil &
    oregano
1 Tbsp. Parmesan
    cheese, grated

Heat skillet, add butter and zucchini, sauté 7-8 minutes. Add remaining ingredients. Serve piping hot.
    Yield: 2 portions

Chicken Jambalaya

2 cut up chicken
    breasts
1/4 cup peanut oil
1 small onion, diced
1 green pepper, cut
    into strips
2 tomatoes in wedges

1/4 tsp. garlic,
    chopped
1/4 tsp. fennel seeds
Salt & pepper
3 cups rice, cooked
2 cups chicken stock
Fresh parsley,
    chopped

Sauté chicken in oil about 5 minutes, add onions, green pepper and garlic, and sauté additional 3-4 minutes stirring frequently. Mix in remaining ingredients and simmer for 20 minutes until almost dry. Serve immediately.
    Yield: 6 portions

EDGAR'S

Looking out across the fairways of The Links celebrity course at Edgar's, you can hear the waves break on the not so distant shore. Head 400 yards toward the ocean and you can walk barefoot in the sand. In this environment I can't think of anything but seafood and vacation!

One look at the golfers, tennis players and club members says resort again and again. This is Wild Dunes, Charleston's island resort on the Isle of Palms. The Links has been ranked the 13th best U.S. resort course by *Golf Digest*. The 17th and 18th holes are rolling fairways edged with soaring, crested dunes and wild sea oats waving in the ocean breeze. It is a Tom Fazio design and is a spectacular course.

Edgar's is on the first floor of The Links Clubhouse. The interior showcases the golf course and seeks to capture the cozy, comfortable feeling of old Charleston. Serving breakfast, lunch and dinner seven days a week, soups, salads and sandwiches are the luncheon fare for the golfer on the go.

Scenes by area artists surround the room creating the perfect setting for a Lowcountry dinner. This is the regional cuisine which draws upon the local bounty of seafood, meat and poultry and local vegetables. The emphasis here clearly is on seafood.

A wide variety of seafood is brought in daily from the charters at the resort marina. The Gulf Stream, about an hour off shore by boat offers many wonderful species of fish. White marlin, blue marlin, wahoo, yellow fin tuna, shark, swordfish, sailfish, bass, trout and tarpon are all caught daily. They find their way to the table either grilled, blackened or broiled .

Seafood Cioppino, with shrimp, scallops, mussels and clams in a tomato broth over pasta is just right after a long day on the links. The Almond Salmon over Warm Spinach Salad is a healthful recipe. Eat seafood and live longer! Just thinking about the tradewinds and what's biting makes me want to hop a john boat or a Carolina skiff and catch my own!

61

Almond Salmon over Warm Spinach Salad

4 salmon filets, pin
 bones & skin removed
Salt & fresh pepper
1 egg
1 cup milk
1 cup almonds, oven
 roasted & chopped
2 Tbsp. olive oil
1 cup red onions, chopped
2 Tbsp. rice wine vinegar
4 Roma tomatoes,
 chopped

1-12 oz. bag fresh
 spinach, cleaned &
 washed
8 pepperoncini
 peppers, chopped
1 cup Kalamata
 olives, seeded
1 cup Feta cheese
 crumbles
1/2 cup fresh basil
 chiffonade *

Lightly season the salmon filets with salt and freshly ground pepper. Beat egg into milk. Coat salmon with small amount of egg wash and sprinkle one side with almonds to form a crust. Place salmon, nut side down in a hot oiled skillet. Turn salmon after it has cooked halfway through and continue cooking the other side until salmon is just pink in the center. Remove salmon filets and set aside in warm oven.

To the same hot skillet, add 2 tablespoons olive oil and sauté the onions for 5 minutes. Add rice vinegar and stir. Add all remaining ingredients and remove from heat. Toss until the spinach is warm and wilted. Portion spinach salad on 4 warm serving plates and top with nut crusted salmon. Eat immediately. Serves 4

*To prepare a basil chiffonade, wash 1/2 pound basil leaves (about 4 cups) in cold water and shake to remove excess water. Cut away and discard the stems and center veins of the leaves. Stack the leaves and slice them very finely. Heat 2 tablespoons of butter in a small heavy saucepan, add the basil, and cook over low heat, stirring once or twice, until the vegetable has melted into a purée, about 10 minutes. Let it cool. Transfer to a covered container and refrigerate until ready to use.

Bourbon Pecan Pie

3 eggs, beaten
1 cup sugar
1 cup dark corn syrup
1/3 cup soft butter
1/4 cup of bourbon

1cup pecans,
    chopped
1/4 cup pecan halves
1-9 inch pie shell,
    unbaked

Preheat oven to 375°.

In a bowl or food processor, mix the eggs, sugar, syrup, butter and bourbon until smooth. Sprinkle the pie shell evenly with chopped pecans. Carefully pour in the filling. Coat each of the remaining pecan halves by dipping in the filling, then arrange them on top. Bake for 40 minutes. Cool until set.

Serves 6

Bull Island

Isle of Palms

Sullivans Island *The Pride,*
Fort Sumter *a three masted gaff schooner sails along the Carolina Coast.*

Cooper River
CHARLESTON
Ashley River
Johns Island
Kiawah Island
Seabrook Island
Edisto River
Edisto Island

Intracoastal

Eighty Two Queen

64

With a name that tells you clearly where to find it, 82 Queen lets you breathe in the pride and tradition of the South. The restaurant, located in the heart of Charleston, is within walking distance of the Public Market, Waterfront Park, the antique shops on King street and the Omni Hotel. With able feet and a good pair of shoes, you can easily make it to the Battery.

82 Queen heralds majestic cuisine and boasts an ambiance all its own. Originally built as three separate single family homes in 1869, it offers a delightful choice of settings. The entry is a small bar that is always full of convivial people. Cozy rooms adjoin it and almost all areas overlook the garden. In the evening the dining rooms are flushed with soft pinks and candlelight.

From March through October both open and covered settings are enticing in the garden. Warmed with greenery and rose pink stucco walls, soft jazzy music plays in the background. An ancient Magnolia tree reigns over the courtyard and turn of the century landscaping has been preserved. Ah! It's such a lovely place to dine and linger awhile. A romantic gazebo, the flickering of gas lights and the hum of overhead ceiling fans issue an intoxicating invitation to luxuriate on a Southern night.

82 Queen, representing the best of the Lowcountry, reflects the flavor and flair of the low lying area surrounding Charleston. Voted Charleston's best restaurant by Charlestonians, 82 Queen has accomplished no mean achievement as the locals are a persnickety lot! Fresh seafood, a medley of salads, and Lowcountry dishes are served with a continental presentation. The Queen is most gracious in that not only lunch and dinner are served, but also a late night supper for theatergoers. The wine list is extensive and while it includes some rare vintages of 1928 with appropriate prices, don't let that scare you away as house wine is also available.

Fabulous specialities change frequently, so ask your waiter's suggestion for the best taste surprise. A raw bar is open in season and is a feast of steamed oysters, clams, fresh oysters and caviar. Don't miss out on the fresh

Chilled Cucumber Soup and Crab Meat Broil as appetizers. The crab recipe is terrific party food or great for a luncheon. When you make the tantalizing Toogoodoo Shrimp and Vegetables in parchment paper, folks will think you rival Martha Stewart!

When the schools of shad fish are running past Charleston in late February and March, marvels come forth from the kitchen! More properly labeled "Shad en Papillotte," at 82 Queen, it's "Shad in a bag!" If you love seafood, ask your waiter what's "running past Charleston" and you're sure to get the freshest catch of the day.

Asparagus and Wild Mushroom Salad

2 lb. fresh asparagus	1 large sweet red pepper
1 cup wild mushrooms (shitake or oyster)	1 small red onion
	1 cup creamy pepper dressing

Clean and cut asparagus into 1 inch pieces. Poach in simmering water for 1 minute. Julienne red pepper into 1 inch pieces. Dice red onion. Mix all the ingredients together and let marinade for 1 hour. Yield: 12 servings

Creamy Pepper Dressing

1 cup mayonnaise	1 tsp. lemon juice
1/2 cup milk	1 tsp. cider vinegar
1 Tbsp. black pepper	1 tsp. Worchestershire
1 Tbsp. Parmesan cheese	1 tsp. garlic, chopped
1 Tbsp. onion, chopped	1/4 tsp. Tabasco sauce

Mix all ingredients together well.
Yield: 2 cups

Oysters Elizabeth

12 oysters on half shell
1 cup spinach,
  cooked and chopped
1/2 cup white crabmeat
1/4 cup sautéed onion,
  finely chopped
1/4 cup cracker meal

3 tsp. mayonnaise
1/2 tsp. dry mustard
1 tsp. Worcestershire
1 tsp. lemon juice
Salt and Pepper to taste
Dash of Tabasco

Blanch spinach in boiling water 10 seconds. Drain and chop. Add all remaining ingredients, tossing gently. Stuff oysters and top with melted butter. Bake in hot oven 5-7 minutes.

Serve with lemon wedges and cocktail sauce.

Yield: 2 appetizer portions

Grilled Clams
with a Garlic Chive Butter

1 lb. butter, softened to
  room temperture
1/4 cup fresh chives,
  chopped
1 lemon (juice only)

1 Tbsp. fresh garlic,
  chopped
1/2 tsp. salt
1/2 tsp. white pepper
12 cherry stone clams

Mix all ingredients, except the clams, in mixing bowl by hand or with electric mixer. Store in airtight container. Keeps up to 3 weeks. Open fresh clams with clam knife. Discard half of the shell. Stuff clams with about 1 teaspoon of garlic chive butter. Place clams on hot open face gas or charcoal grill. Cook until butter is melted and bubbling hot.

Yield: 2 appetizer portions

McClellanville Crab Cakes served over a bed of Sweet Red Pepper Cream

1 lb. lump crabmeat	1 dash of Worcestershire
1/2 cup mayonnaise	sauce
2 dashes of Tabasco	1/2 cup coarse bread
2 green onions, chopped fine	crumbs
1/2 oz. fresh lemon juice	1/2 tsp. ground thyme

Combine ingredients thoroughly, then form into desired cake size, about 4 ounces.

Make egg wash of 2 eggs and 1/4 cup half & half. Dip cakes in egg mixture, then roll in more bread crumbs. Sauté in butter or olive oil until golden brown.

Yield: 6 cakes

Sweet Red Pepper Cream

4 large sweet red peppers seeded, and diced medium	3 tsp. honey
	1/2 tsp. white pepper
3 large shallots, peeled and chopped	1 tsp. apple cider vinegar
1/2 cup water	1 tsp. cilantro, chopped

Sauté pepper and shallots together in a little oil. Add 1/2 cup water and simmer 20 minutes or until peppers are soft completely through.

Using a high speed blender, place peppers, shallots and all remaining ingredients, except cilantro, in a bowl, blending until smooth. Run through a medium strainer. Add cilantro and set aside at room temperature.

Yield: 10 portions

Toogoodoo Vegetables and Shrimp in Parchment Paper

4 doz. large shrimp, peeled and deveined
1 small Vidalia onion
1 sweet red bell pepper
1/4 cup fresh herbs (basil dill, cilantro, tarragon)

1 Tbsp. black pepper
1 small yellow squash
16 pieces of fresh okra
1/2 cup olive oil
Salt to taste

Preheat over to 400°.

Cut all vegetables into medium size sticks. Toss all ingredients in large mixing bowl. Divide vegetables and shrimp onto 4 pieces of parchment paper and fold paper over. Fold edges, making sure completely sealed. Bake for 15-20 minutes.

Yield: 4 portions

Maison Du Pré, The Inn of Historic Elegance, c. 1804
317 East Bay St., Charleston, S.C.

Death by Chocolate

Crust:

7 Tbsp. margarine, melted	1 cup pecans, chopped
1/2 cup graham cracker crumbs	1 tsp. cinnamon

Preheat oven to 325°.

Mix well and press in the bottom of a 9 inch springform pan. Bake for 8 minutes and cool.

Filling:

2 sticks butter	1/2 box powdered sugar
1 Tbsp. cornstarch	6 large eggs
1 Tbsp. vanilla	1/4 cup whipping cream
18 oz. semi-sweet chocolate chips, melted	

Preheat oven to 350°.

Soften butter slightly in large bowl in microwave (about 1/3 to 1/2 way melted) for 3 minutes on LOW. Mix butter (with electric mixer) with powdered sugar, vanilla and cornstarch. Melt chocolate chips in microwave in separate bowl until it stirs smooth. Pour into butter mixture and mix together well, then add eggs: mix in 3 at a time, mixing well. Next add whipping cream, blending well. Pour into crust and bake for 10 minutes. Cool in refrigerator about 6 hours before cutting from pan.

Banana Foster

1 banana, cut into strips	1 Tbsp. light brown
2 Tbsp. butter	sugar
1 oz. dark rum	1/2 fresh orange

In a saucepan, melt butter and sugar: add banana sections and sauté 1 minute. Turn over and add rum and juice from orange. Yield: 1 serving

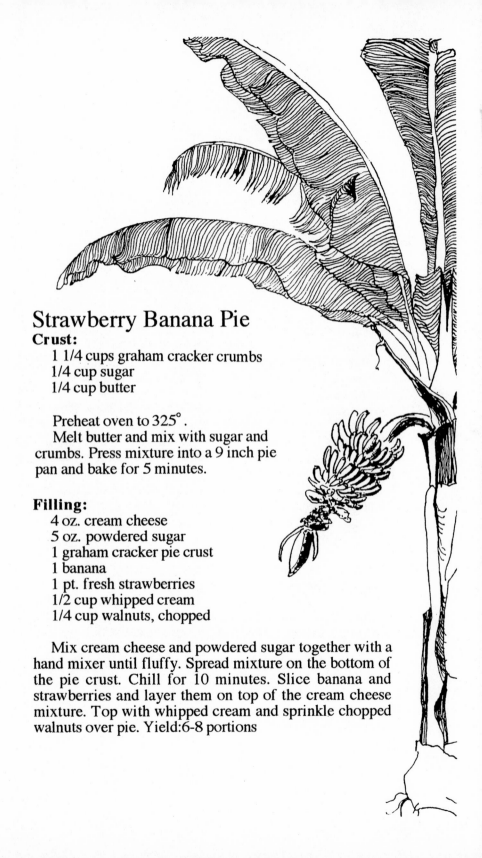

Strawberry Banana Pie
Crust:
> 1 1/4 cups graham cracker crumbs
> 1/4 cup sugar
> 1/4 cup butter

Preheat oven to 325°.
Melt butter and mix with sugar and crumbs. Press mixture into a 9 inch pie pan and bake for 5 minutes.

Filling:
> 4 oz. cream cheese
> 5 oz. powdered sugar
> 1 graham cracker pie crust
> 1 banana
> 1 pt. fresh strawberries
> 1/2 cup whipped cream
> 1/4 cup walnuts, chopped

Mix cream cheese and powdered sugar together with a hand mixer until fluffy. Spread mixture on the bottom of the pie crust. Chill for 10 minutes. Slice banana and strawberries and layer them on top of the cream cheese mixture. Top with whipped cream and sprinkle chopped walnuts over pie. Yield:6-8 portions

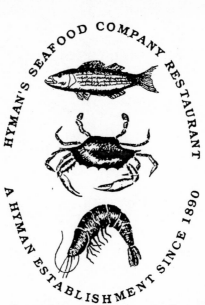

HYMAN'S SEAFOOD COMPANY RESTAURANT · A HYMAN ESTABLISHMENT SINCE 1890

Come away from the great houses on the grand tour and step into another legendary world in Charleston. Hyman's is home to the Original Charleston 13 Bean Soup. This is tradition at its finest. If you haven't tasted this soup, you haven't tasted Charleston!

Great grandfather Hyman came to America from Russia as a small boy in the 1800's. He worked the streets of Charleston as a peddler before becoming a wholesale dry goods seller in a building down the street from the present Hyman's. In 1890 he was the first distributor of Hanes underwear in the Southeast. The former location on Meeting Street burned in a fire in 1973 and Hyman's Seafood moved to the Victorian building it is presently in. The old English bricks are set with the original oyster mortar. With heart pine floors, and cozy tables, the atmosphere is hearty, homey and comforting.

Hyman's is owned by the grandsons Eli and Aaron. Family unity and tradition are the recurring themes of the Hyman family and the brothers have always enjoyed working together. "We both live and breathe this place," says Eli. Uncle Melvin Firetag lends his support as well, meeting and greeting people outside on the sidewalk. You can view the spotless kitchen and witness the zeal for cleanliness and order. The Majority of the customers are local. Legendary Senator Strom Thurmond became a favorite long ago.

The Hyman brothers are wise beyond their years in building customer loyalty. When fame arrived and celebrities such as Oprah, Barbra, Billy Joel, and Baryshnikov became diners, Eli worried that his regular "Folly Beach bunch" would feel slighted by all the crowds. So the names of the faithful "regulars" were printed on the back of the chairs they sat in. As to their civic responsibility the Hyman family mix their own Cajun seasonings and the proceeds from this venture go to the Ronald McDonald House in Charleston, aiding families who have seriously ill children.

Hyman's is home to an award winning She Crab Soup, the original 13 Bean Soup and a great Okra Gumbo. Blackened fish is served straight through from lunch into dinner. Come dinner time, Hyman's has them standing in a line running clear up Meeting Street. Eli and Aaron are quick to tell you they are neither pricy or fancy! They give superior quality and great value.

Charleston 13 Bean Soup

1 lb. 13 mixed beans	3 quarts of water
(black eyed peas, lentils,	1 ham bone
great northern, navy, lima,	1 can stewed tomatoes
pinto, kidney, etc.)	Salt & pepper to taste

1. Wash the beans thoroughly in cold water. Put 3 quarts of water in a soup kettle along with the beans. Heat the beans slowly to a boil and simmer gently for 2 minutes. Turn the heat off and let the beans soak for 2 hours.

2. Add the ham bone, stewed tomatoes, salt and freshly ground pepper to taste. Cover and cook over low heat for 2 1/2 hours, stirring occasionally. Add more water, while cooking, if the soup becomes too thick. Serve with Tabasco sauce on the side.

Yield: 10 cups

Louis's Charleston Grill has become a leader in interpreting regional cuisine. As chef for the elite palates of the Vanderbilts while formerly at Pawley's Island Inn, Louis Osteen gained quite a following. The Omni Hotel enticed Osteen to be chef and creator of his own restaurant. Since opening Louis's Charleston Grill, Osteen has been chosen to prepare a three course dinner of Lowcountry specialities for no less than Prince Charles.

Always low-key, he states simply that he wants to prepare food that is "tasty and good!" A weekly changing menu is centered on regionally themed dishes such as Preserved Duck with Fried Grits. Chef Louis features quail, fragrant peaches and cured local hams. Beyond being a chef, Osteen has launched not only a crayfish industry in the Carolinas, but also The South Carolina Crayfish Festival.

Crayfish Tails and Crabmeat in Caviar Butter is a dish that customers rave about. Risotto with Local Shellfish and Mushrooms was the choice Osteen deemed fit for a Prince. His Grilled Lamb Ribs with Shallot and Pepper Butter received the "Golden Dish" award from *GQ* magazine, and you get to eat them with your fingers! All this can be enjoyed nightly while listening to live jazz! Talk about good!

The handsome grill opens right into the foyer of the hotel. Deep mahogany walls are the background for leather bankettes and old Charleston photos, lending that "always been there" ambiance. This is the place F. Scott and Zelda would frequent. A man in a white linen suit enters looking like Robert Redford with a mustache and wearing a Panama hat. I pick up the scent of bay rum. They say dress is casual, but the place reeks of class and looks like a Ralph Lauren fashion layout should be shot here. Surely this is a meeting place after a day of polo at Boone Hall?

The hotel was named one of the top 25 hotels in America by *Conde Nast Traveler*. Four Star and Diamond and Gold Key are just a few ways to describe the classic proportions and old fashioned Southern hospitality of this grand hotel. Not to be outdone by the Omni's accomplishments, Louis's has been named one of the country's top 25 restaurants by *Esquire* magazine. His recipes have been featured in *Town and Country, Southern Living* and *Bon Appetit,* in addition to receiving the Wine Spectator and Dirona awards. Not bad for a fellow who claims his culinary training is from the "School of Hot Stoves" and had Hurricane Hugo ruin the grand opening by crashing into town!

Dinner served nightly from 6:00 to 11:00, average cost $30-35, jazz at 7:00. Sumptuous Sunday Brunch!

Carolina Pigeon Stewed
with Winter Vegetables

6 squab, with the
  backbone and the rib
  cage removed and the
  leg and thigh bones intact
1/2 lb. bacon cut into
  1/4 inch pieces
6 Tbsp. butter
4 cups shredded
  cabbage blanched
  for three minutes
  in boiling water

1 1/2 cups onions,
  sliced
1 1/2 cups carrot,
  cut into 1/4 inch slices
1 1/2 cups parsnips,
  pared and cut into
  1/4 inch slices
2 cups dry red wine
2 cups chicken broth
Salt and pepper to taste

For the Stuffing:

3 cups wild rice, cooked
  then chilled
2 Tbsp. shallot, minced

2 Tbsp. chive, minced
1 Tbsp. melted butter
Salt and pepper

Toss all of the stuffing ingredients together and refrigerate until ready to use.

Stuff and truss the squab.

In a heavy skillet, sauté the bacon in the butter. Remove the bacon when it is browned and reserve for later use. Quickly brown the squab on all sides. In the same fat (if the fat is burned, wipe the skillet clean and add new) sauté the vegetables until they are beginning to color. Empty the vegetables into a strainer in order to dispose of the used fat. Replace the vegetables in the sauté pan and add wine and stock. Let the vegetables simmer slowly, partially covered for 30 minutes. Place the squab on the vegetables and lightly press them into the vegetables. The squab should be about half submerged into the wine and vegetables. This way the legs and thighs will cook in the moist heat and the breasts will roast. Baste the breasts every 10 minutes with a few spoonfuls of the cooking liquid. After 20 minutes, remove the squab to a warmed platter and let rest in a warm, quiet place while finishing. Quickly place the vegetables and remaining cooking juices onto a warmed serving platter and top with the squab.

Yield: 3-6 portions

Ravenel Gaillard

Risotto with Local Shellfish and Mushrooms

3 Tbsp. olive oil
2 Tbsp. butter
1 cup onions, chopped
4 cups Amborio rice
1/2 cup fresh fennel, chopped
8-10 cups of hot chicken or fish stock
1 cup shrimp, peeled and deveined

1/2 cup raw scallops
1/2 cup shucked clams
1 cup mushrooms (a combination of whatever is available), sautéed
4 Tbsp. parsley, thyme and olives, minced
2 tbsp. minced fennel

In a heavy saucepan, heat the oil and butter. Add onion and cook until transparent. Add rice and fennel. Cook until the rice is opaque. Begin adding the stock 1/2 cup at a time. Stir rice continuously as stock is absorbed, adding another 1/2 cup as precious stock is absorbed. After the third stock addition, add shellfish and mushrooms. Continue adding stock until all is used. After the last addition of the stock, add herbs. The risotto should be almost chewey and a little firm in the center. Serve immediately.

Yield: 8 portions

Crawfish Tails and Crabmeat in Caviar Butter Sauce

1/4 cup fish stock
1/3 cup vermouth
1 Tbsp. white wine vinegar
2 Tbsp. shallots, chopped
Fresh black pepper
1/2 lb. unsalted butter softened and divided

4 tbsp. fresh sturgeon caviar
3/4 lb. fresh crawfish tails, cooked and peeled
3/4 lb. fresh jumbo lump crabmeat

Combine fish stock, vermouth, wine vinegar, shallots and black pepper in a medium saucepan and cook over medium heat until mixture is reduced to four tablespoons.

Add 1/4 lb. of butter, piece by piece, whisking thoroughly after each addition. Continue to whip until the mixture boils and becomes thick and creamy. Stir in 2 tablespoons of the caviar, cover pan and keep warm.

In a small skillet, stew crawfish tails in remaining 1/4 lb. butter over very low heat. Toss gently until warmed through. Add crabmeat and cook only to heat mixture thoroughly.

Place seafood mixture on warmed plates and ladle the warm caviar butter overall. Garnish with remaining caviar. Yield: 4 portions

Buttermilk Tart
with Fresh Raspberries

1 dough for pie crust
2 1/2 cups sugar
3 Tbsp. all purpose flour
3 large eggs
5 Tbsp. unsalted butter
   melted and cooled
1 1/2 cups buttermilk

1 tsp. pure vanilla
   extract
1 tsp. red wine
   vinegar
1 1/2 pints fresh
   raspberries
1 cup tart glaze or jelly

Prepare plain pastry and line a "12" tart pan with a removable bottom. "Flute" the crust all around the rim and prick the entire surface with a fork to remove any air bubbles. Cover the bottom of the shell with dried beans to weight crust. Bake at 450° for 15-18 minutes.

In a large bowl, mix the sugar and flour. In another bowl, mix all of the wet ingredients. Combine the two and mix well but try not to incorporate any air into the mixture. Pour the filling into the baked pie shell and bake at 370° until lightly browned and the tart is set in the middle. Let cool to room temperature. Cover the tart completly with raspberries. Gently brush with warmed glaze. Yield: 6 portions

Magnolias ®

Uptown
Down South

Yes, it is Uptown, but my oh my, it sure is down South! Magnolia's, the city's most celebrated restaurant, has been lauded for both elegance and cuisine by *Southern Living, Travel and Leisure* and *Bon Appetit*. It is only one of five restaurants in South Carolina to receive the sought after Dirona award. Standing at 185 Bay Street on Lodge Alley, is in the heart of Charleston's oldest district and just a breeze away from the harbor.

A map dated 1739 marks this stellar location as Charleston's original custom house. Lodge Alley is one of the oldest streets in Charleston and was within the original "Walled City." During the colonial period, this area teemed with activity by the early French settlers who worked the docks fronting on what is now East Bay Street. The industrious Huguenots thrived in this bustling port, and the area became known as the "French Quarter District. "

The "Alley" dining room at the entrance looks right out on Bay Street and Lodge Alley through large sun-splashed windows by day. Opposite is the horse-shoe shaped Veranda bar made from antique heartpine. The "Chef's Room" looks right into the kitchen with a flurry of activity and flows into still another more elegant, elevated room. Throughout, all the walls are studded with bold signature paintings of magnolias created by Rod Goebel. Classic architectural features of columns, marble floors, and warm rich woods combined with an open sense of space creates an effect that is both old and new.

Magnolia'a Uptown/Down South decor has established a new style in town. Blending historic charm and contemporary excitement, Magnolia's is definitely unlike any other in Charleston and has quickly became the town's hot spot. The objective from the beginning was to present local ingredients with a twist. Chef Donald Barickman, a graduate of the Culinary Institute of America wanted to bring a kind of fresh taste but one true to the restaurant's name. A diverse menu is one of contemporary American cuisine with a southern flavor. Barickman's influences are France, Italy, Cajun, South Carolina Upstate and the Pacific Rim.

Charlestonians eat shrimp any time of day and a favorite is the Spicy Shrimp and Sausage over Creamy Grits. A popular menu item is a Grilled Salmon over Creamy Grits with Dill and Shallot Butter. Grit Cakes with Tasso Gravy is another favorite. (Tasso is Cajun ham.) All pastry and desserts are baked fresh and are heavenly. You could live on their breads alone! Their wine list is innovative with many fine wines available by the glass. The restaurant runs an "California Exclusive" list offering a chance to try wines from small vineyards that are not available elsewhere.

Magnolia's is frequented by the stars of films being made hereabouts. Demi Moore, Anthony Hopkins, Nick Nolte, Kevin Costner and the "Sweet Justice" crew came to feast! This is a great place to people-watch! Ask your waiter! (Great service!) Magnolia's is open seven days a week serving continuously from lunch through dinner.

Spicy Shrimp and Sausage
over Creamy White Grits with Tasso Gravy

Creamy Grits:
2 quarts chicken broth (double strength preferred)
2 1/2 cups coarse ground white grits
1 cup heavy cream
Salt and pepper

Bring the chicken stock to a boil in a heavy-bottomed pot. Rinse the grits and slowly stir into the boiling chicken stock. Bring back to a boil then lower the heat and stir very frequently for 25-30 minutes. The grits should have absorbed all of the chicken stock and become soft. Add the heavy cream and cook an additional 20 minutes, stirring frequently so it won't scorch. Season with salt and pepper and keep warm in a double boiler until ready for service. If the grits become too thick add warm water or cream to thin them down.

Tasso Gravy:

2 oz. whole butter   1 quart chicken stock
1/2 cup all purpose flour   3 oz. tasso ham

In a heavy bottomed pot, melt the butter and add the flour to make a roux. Cook over very low heat for 3-5 minutes or until it has a nutty aroma. Slowly but gradually add the cold chicken stock stirring constantly with a whip. Increase the heat to high and continue stirring until the gravy comes to a boil. It is important at this time to get out all the lumps by whisking briskly. The gravy should simmer for 10-15 minutes to cook out any starchy flavor. Add the tasso ham and hold for service. Tasso gravy can be made in advance, add tasso when ready for service.

Shrimp and Sausage:

4 oz. per person of Italian sausage
4 oz. medium sized shrimp, peeled and deveined
1/2 oz. per person of heavy cream
1/2 bunch of parsley, chopped

It is best to bake off the sausage ahead of time and cut into small pieces when cooled.

Sauté shrimp in butter or olive oil, add the sausage. Ladle the tasso gravy into the pan with the shrimp and sausage, cook 1-2 minutes. Add the heavy cream and continue to cook another minute. If the gravy is too thick, thin down with water or chicken stock.

Portion creamy grits into a bowl about 8 oz. Spoon shrimp and sausage mixture over grits and sprinkle with chopped parsley. Serve at once.

Ravenel Gaillard

The Sword Gate   Robert Sillers

Skillet Seared Yellow Grits
with Tasso Gravy

1 qt. chicken broth   1 cup heavy cream
2 1/2 cups yellow grits,   2 oz. whole butter
   coarse ground

1. Rinse grits.
2. Bring chicken stock and butter to a boil and stir in grits. Reboil, then stir occasionally to keep grits from settling to the bottom and scorching.
3. Cool about 30 minutes over a very low heat (stirring frequently).
4. Add heavy cream and cook another 20 minutes.
5. Season to taste with salt and white pepper.
6. Pour into a one inch deep pan lined with parchment paper. The grits should be a thick mass, not runny.
7. Spread to 1 inch thick and let cool until firm.
8. Cut into a desired shape and dust with cornmeal. Pan fry until crispy, and place in oven until warm throughout.
9. For tasso gravy, see previous recipe.

84

Lemon Lingonberry Vinaigrette

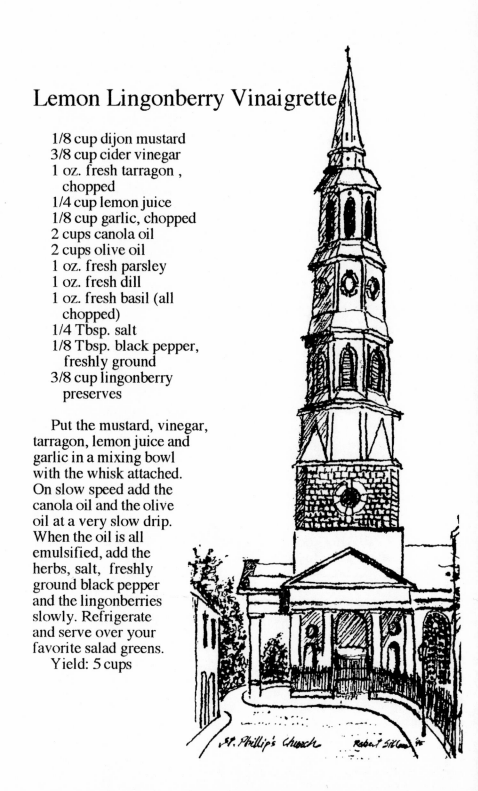

1/8 cup dijon mustard
3/8 cup cider vinegar
1 oz. fresh tarragon ,
   chopped
1/4 cup lemon juice
1/8 cup garlic, chopped
2 cups canola oil
2 cups olive oil
1 oz. fresh parsley
1 oz. fresh dill
1 oz. fresh basil (all
   chopped)
1/4 Tbsp. salt
1/8 Tbsp. black pepper,
   freshly ground
3/8 cup lingonberry
   preserves

Put the mustard, vinegar, tarragon, lemon juice and garlic in a mixing bowl with the whisk attached. On slow speed add the canola oil and the olive oil at a very slow drip. When the oil is all emulsified, add the herbs, salt, freshly ground black pepper and the lingonberries slowly. Refrigerate and serve over your favorite salad greens.
   Yield: 5 cups

St. Phillip's Church   Robert Sillon '95

Cream Cheese Brownie
with Ice Cream and Chocolate Sauce

8 oz. sweet chocolate	1 tbsp. vanilla
6 oz. butter	1 tsp. baking powder
6 oz. cream cheese, softened	1/2 tsp. salt
2 cups sugar	1 cup English walnuts, chopped
6 eggs	1/4 tsp. almond extract
1 1/4 cups flour	

1. Melt the chocolate with 3 oz. of the butter, over a double boiler, remove and let cool to room temperature.

2. Cream the remaining 3 oz. of butter with the cream cheese, gradually add 1/2 cup of the sugar, then blend in 2 eggs, 2 tablespoons of flour and 1 tablespoon vanilla, set aside.

3. Beat the 4 eggs until opaque, gradually add the 1 1/2 cups of remaining sugar and the baking powder mixed together then add the salt and remaining flour. Stir in the melted chocolate mixture in Step 1. Add the nuts, and the rest of the vanilla extract and almond extract.

4. Pour the chocolate batter into a greased 8 X 12 cake pan and fold in the cream cheese batter.

5. Bake at 350°, 35-40 minutes.

6. After cooling, cut the brownies into squares and top with your favorite ice cream and drizzle with warm Chocolate Sauce.

Chocolate Sauce:

4 oz. sweet chocolate	1 cup heavy cream
2 oz. butter	

Melt together in a double boiler and serve warm.

Church Street   The Eveleigh House   Robert Sillers

Marianne is an intimately decorated little French charmer housed in several buildings on Meeting Street. Since opening many years ago, it has become a Charleston tradition in French cooking. Marianne's chef Serge Clair hails from Vichy and served his apprenticeship at La Pyramide. Any Frenchman will tell you, that in the world of culinary arts, starting at La Pyramide is starting at the top.

The French Huguenots came to Charleston around 1681. Their influence on the architecture is present along the Battery, the city's harbor area. Buildings made of stucco and hipped roofs are as much in evidence as are mansard roofs, overhanging balconies and convex tiles, all characteristic of France. These early settlers founded the first and still existing French Huguenot church which adheres to the original French liturgy. Despite the influence of the French on the city, until the advent of Marianne, there was not one French restaurant.

Only moderately expensive, you may have a table d' hote dinner or enjoy choosing from an a la carte menu. The recipe for a great appetizer, Mushrooms Stuffed With Crabmeat, was generously given as well as the Veal Cristo served with a Ratatouille. This is a dish of eggplant, tomatoes, onions and zucchini. Omit the veal and you have an excellent vegetarian dinner. The menu includes the traditional Coq au vin, Rack of Lamb, Chateaubriand, Pâté, and crisp salads. A favorite is La Charlestonaisse Bouilliabaisse! Tres bien! The French Society meets here! The pastries are made fresh daily and whether it's a tempting Triple Chocolate Terrine, a Fresh Fruit Tart, Bananas Foster or a Chestnut Mousse, my advise is to choose at least one!

Dinner begins at 6:00 nightly with late night suppers served for those who celebrate when the night is young! A piano plays Broadway favorites. My thanks to Serge for his anecdotes, his tips on a better bordelaise and his tales of the French Foreign Legion. Everyone says the French know how to eat, but I say they know how to live and savor life. Viva la Marianne!

Ratatouille

1 lb. eggplant	1 yellow onion
4 large zucchini	2 cloves garlic
4 large ripe tomatoes	6 Tbsp. olive oil
1 large green pepper	Salt & fresh pepper

Wash and trim the eggplant and zucchini but do not peel them. Cut them into 1/4-inch-thick slices. Salt lightly and let them drain in a colander for 1 hour. Peel the tomatoes and chop them coarsely. Wash, seed, derib and cut up the flesh of the pepper. Peel and coarsely chop the onion and garlic.

Heat the olive oil in a large skillet or casserole. Sauté the onion and garlic for about 5 minutes over a low heat until transparent. Add the peppers and cook for another ten minutes. Add all the remaining vegetables and season to taste with salt and freshly ground pepper.

Cover tightly and cook over a low heat, stirring occasionally, for one hour or until thick and well blended. This outstanding vegetable dish can be served hot or cold

Yield: 6-8 portions

La Charlestonaisse Bouillabaisse

4 lbs. fish (snapper, salmon, grouper)
3 lbs. shellfish (mussels, scallops, crab, clams, shrimp)
1/2 cup olive oil
2 large yellow onions
3 leeks (white part only)
2 cups white wine
2 1/2 quarts fish stock
4 tomatoes (peeled)

2 oz. parsley, chopped
1/8 tsp. saffron
1/8 tsp. fennel powder
1/4 tsp. fennel leaves
1 bay leaf
1 sprig savory
1 pinch thyme
1/2 oz. pernod
2 tsp. salt
10 slices French bread
5 oz. butter

Comments: La Charlestonaisse is a local version of the ever popular bouillabaisse, a French specialty. At Marianne Restaurant we use whatever fresh local fish and shellfish that are available.

1. Slice the onions and leeks and sauté them in olive oil.
2. Combine all the remaining ingredients except for the fish, shellfish and French bread and simmer for 20 minutes.
3. Add fish and simmer for 10 minutes.
4. Add all the shellfish and simmer for 5 minutes more.
5. Toast bread and brush with garlic butter, place on bottom of soup bowl, pour the soup over the bread and serve.
Yield: 10 portions

Crabmeat in Mushroom Caps

Béchamel Sauce:

4 Tbsp. butter	1 cup half & half
4 Tbsp. flour	1 cup milk

Heat butter in a saucepan, stir in the flour and cook for 2-3 minutes. Add the half & half and milk gradually while stirring. Bring the sauce to a boil, stirring or beating well until smooth. Cook for additional 15 minutes until thickened. Set aside.

Crabmeat Filling:

2 Tbsp. butter	1/2 cup white wine
3 little shallots, chopped fine	24 large mushrooms
1/2 lb. crabmeat	Salt & fresh pepper
	Half of a lemon

In a skillet melt the butter and sauté the shallots just until they begin to brown. Gently drop in the crabmeat and turn with a wooden spatula. Add the white wine and cook until it begins to boil, then season with salt and fresh pepper to taste. Pour the béchamel sauce over the crabmeat and mix until unified. Allow this mixture to cool.

Place uncooked mushroom caps in a buttered dish. Mound each cap with the crabmeat mixture. Give each mound a squeeze of lemon juice, a dab of butter and just a touch of salt and fresh pepper.

Pop in the oven at 450° for 10 minutes!

Yield: 6 portions

Mussels Marianne

4 lbs. mussels
  in shells
1 cup white wine
1 large yellow
  onion, minced
5 shallots, minced

1 clove garlic,
  minced
2 pints heavy cream
1 cup fresh parsley,
  chopped
Salt & fresh pepper

Comments: Wash the mussels thoroughly, using a stiff brush to scrub the shells and remove the beard. Discard any that are open. Rinse with cold running water until there is no trace of sand.

1. In a seperate pot, reduce heavy cream by half, set aside until later.

2. Sauté garlic, shallots and onion until translucent, in a large pot.

3. Add white wine, leave pot uncovered, cook until wine is reduced by half.

4. Add mussels, salt and freshly ground pepper.

5. Cover the pot and shake until mussels are covered.

6. Add chopped parsley.

7. Add reserved reduced cream.

8. Shake again until sauce covers all mussels.

9. Recover and cook until mussels start to open.

10. Leave covered and remove from heat, but allow to steam open.

Serving suggestions: A great appetizer, serve with hot French bread for dipping and a nice Cotes du Rhone for sipping.

Yield: 8 portions

Papaya-Cream Cheese Tart with Macadamia Nuts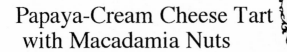

2 cups flour
1/4 tsp. salt
1/2 tsp. sugar
6 oz. very cold
  unsalted butter cut
  into 1/2 inch cubes
1/3 cup cold water
12 oz. cream cheese
4 oz. heavy cream,
  whipped to
  soft peaks
1/2 cup powdered
  sugar
1/2 tsp. vanilla

1 very ripe papaya,
  peeled and sliced
  into 1/4 " slices
11/2 cup peach glaze
  or jam, melted
1/2 c. macadamia
  nuts, toasted
8 oz. bitter chocolate
8 oz. semisweet
  chocolate
2 1/2 cups
  heavy cream
4 Tbsp. warm water

Prepare the tart shell:

Sift together the flour, salt, and sugar. Coat butter cubes with the flour mixture and water and knead until malleable, but not homogeneous. (The amount of water given is approximate: adjust the amount used according to the dough's consistency.) Leave bits of plain butter, otherwise the dough become too elastic. Gently roll dough to 1/4 inch thickness and lay onto a tart pan. Trim edges and poke bottom of pastry with a fork. Bake in oven at 350° for about 10 minutes or until tart shell browns slightly. Chill.

Prepare cream cheese filling:

· Whip heavy cream until it forms soft peaks. In a mixer, beat cream cheese until it becomes fluffy. Fold in whipped cream, powdered sugar and vanilla extract. Set aside.

Assemble Tart:

Fill tart shell with cream cheese mixture. Arrange papaya slices in a pinwheel desigh over the top of the cream cheese. Place macadamia nuts in center of tart. With a pastry brush, coat top of tart with peach glaze. Refrigerate for 1/2 hour before serving.

Chocolate Sauce:

Heat bitter chocolate, semisweet chocolate, heavy cream and warm water in a saucepan, stirring frequently, until sauce is a smooth consistency.

To serve:

Slice tart into 8 pieces. Drizzle chocolate sauce onto plate and place one piece of tart on each plate.

Serves 8

MIDDLETON PLACE
RESTAURANT

To most people, just to mention the word plantation, will bring to mind vast reaches of lush green land studded with huge, sprawling live oak trees, a grand house, and heaping platters of food. Margaret Mitchell gave the world an indelible image of this way of life that today has all but been erased. Middleton Place preserves a past and makes the stuff of legends a living reality.

96

Middleton Place, a Registered National Landmark, offers a varied spectrum of plantation life as it was in a bygone era. It lies fourteen miles northwest of Charleston. Within the landmark area are the famed gardens, the 1755 House, the plantation stableyards outdoor museum, a beautiful museum shop, and a one-of-a-kind restaurant serving Lowcountry fare.

There is only one place to dine in Charleston that is set in the middle of a 250 year old historic plantation! The Middleton Place Restaurant is settled into one of the many beautiful old buildings that grace the plantation grounds. It is a faithful replica of the plantation's original rice mill and was designed by W. Bancel LeFarge. After a sojourne in Barbadoes he was inspired to begin the work in 1933.

Originally built as as a guest house, the restaurant began as a tea room introduced by the Junior League in the late 1940's. The deep, rich, pecky cypress planks used in the walls was grown on the grounds. The warmth and ragged character of these rarely seen woods combine with a great fireplace to create a welcoming atmosphere. Favorite seating in Spring is on the enclosed porch with a heavenly view of vibrant azaleas running rampant along the banks of the mill pond. No visit to Charleston is complete without a trip to Middleton. The view of the oldest landscaped gardens in America right across your table is an attraction impossible to equal.

The menu serves true plantation fare and delivers the promise of authenticity. Respected Southern Chef Edna Lewis left behind her influence when she trained Audrey Aiken as head chef. It is Edna's recipes that are used in the day and evening menu selection to maintain the purity of plantation fare. And talk about fresh, everything is grown locally or swam in local waters!

Chefs from across the country were asked to choose their personal favorite chefs in a survey by American Airlines. Published in their *American Way* magazine, they selected Middleton Place as a top ten restaurant representing American cuisine at its finest. They lauded Edna Lewis as the "greatest living practitioner of old fashioned Southern cooking" among such highly visible chefs as Paul Prudhomme of New Orleans and Spago's Wolfgang Puck in Los Angeles. About time an icon of Southern cooking was recognized. My special thanks to Audrey Aiken and Paula Evans, Director of Food Services, who make Middleton deserving of such accolades for its richness of character, great food and hospitality.

With luncheon specialities of Hoppin' John and Ham Biscuits, Okra Gumbo and She-Crab Soup served daily from 11:00 to 3:00, the meaning of plantation fare is revealed. Not too long ago gumbo was made with rabbit and even a possum or a squirrel if your gun was handy. Today many gumbos are made with chicken or shrimp or sausage, but this one is totally vegetarian! Its a terrific recipe and suitable for our health conscious way of life. Sea Island shrimp, barbecued pork, field peas, corn pudding, collards and corn bread are samplings from the midday menu.

From 3:00 to 4:30 drinks are available with a full bar, and luscious desserts! Spoon Bread is a requirement to be able to walk away and declare that you have tasted plantation food! Not to be missed is that toothsome historic dessert with the "receipt" dating back to the French court of Henry IV! The French Protestants found a taste of heaven when they created the Huguenot Torte!

Dinner is served Friday and Saturday evenings from 5:00 to 9:00. Entrees of Panned Quail with Ham will make your mouth-water when it comes to the table. Broiled Oysters, Breast of Chicken, Beef or Pork Tenderloin, Fresh Flounder, and Sea Scallops provide a bountiful feast. Thus satisfied and contented, all the better able you'll be to enjoy this lush paradise.

Gardens ~ House ~ Stableyards
Registered National Historic Landmark

   Majestic is the only word to describe Middleton Place
Gardens. The oldest landscaped gardens in America cover
over 60 acres of the plantation. Their outstanding design
is a study of artistic balance and form reminiscent of the
eighteenth century gardens of Europe. Their lavish
formality was laid out in 1741 by Henry Middleton. Work
continueed for a decade to sculpt what was originally a
bluff above the river into a fantasy of magnificent
rolling terraces that descend to identically proportioned
"butterfly lakes" and continue down to the famous Ashley
River.

Open all year the gardens offer a calendar of color. In April the azaleas, Cherokee rose and dogwood are at their peak. The mountain laurel holds reign in May, and summer brings the day lilies, crepe myrtle, roses, and the sweeping fragrance of the tea olive. In 1787 the great French botanist Andre Michaux introduced the Camelia Japonica whose soft beauty graces the gardens during the winter months. Middleton is famed for these as well as its mighty live oaks, one of which is 900 years old!

The plantation stableyards are an outdoor museum of animals and farm implements. It chronicles the rise and fall of the rice and cotton eras. Demonstrations bring to life yesteryears' crafts that were all a part of the day to day life of the 18th and 19th century plantation. The expert craftsmen demonstrate the skills of blacksmithing, carpentry, tanning, coopering, and soap making from lye and potash. Turn the hand-operated millstone used to make grits from corn a few times, and you'll realize the stamina necessary for survival in another century!

The 6,500 acre plantation sets on the tidal banks of the Ashley River which helped Middleton to flourish in the cultivation of rice. Milling is the first step in rice processing. Coopers fashioned the barrels for the storage and shipment of rice grown on the plantation. The blacksmith fashioned the barrel hoops that held the barrels together during shipments across the Atlantic.

The land was first settled in the late 17th century, and was acquired by Henry Middleton through marriage in 1741. The family left an indelible imprint on American history. Henry Middleton was President of the First Continental Congress and was succeeded by his son Arthur who was one of the signers of the Declaration of Independence. His son Williams Middleton was a signer of the Ordinance of Secession, that famous statement of withdrawal from the Union by 11 Southern states in the years 1860-61. During the War Between the States, as Charlestonians call it, the house was put to the torch by Sherman's Union forces. After the Civil War, the gardens fell to disrepair. They remained neglected until 1916 when restoration began.

The Middleton House is so beautiful it is overwhelming to think it is only a wing of the original main house. Throughout it lies a visible evolving tale of both family and American history: books, silver, family portraits by Benjamin West and a breakfast table by the Charlestonian cabinet maker of the mid-1700's Thomas Elfe. Outstanding are the 4-poster rice beds made over 200 years ago, and rare documents in a library including a silk copy of the Declaration of Independence!

Annual events include the Sheep to Shawl demonstration in April, Starlight Pops in May, Plantation Days in November and lovely Christmas celebrations. None surpasses the Spoleto Finale in June when seemingly all of Charleston descends to see this wondrous event unfold ceremoniously on the banks of the Ashley.

Middleton Place Biscuits

1 lb. all purpose flour
2 tsp. salt
2 Tbsp. baking powder

4 oz. shortening
1 cup plus 2 tbsp. buttermilk

Preheat oven to 450°.

Put the flour, salt, baking powder and shortening in a mixing bowl. Blend with pastry blender or use your fingertips until the mixture is the texture of cornmeal. Add buttermilk all at once and stir for a few seconds.

Work dough into a ball and turn onto a lightly floured surface. Knead dough, then shape the dough into a round cake. Dust rolling pin and rolling surface lightly with flour.

Roll dough evenly from center outward into a 1/4 inch thickness. Cut out biscuits using a 2 1/2 inch cutter dipped in flour. Press straight down and pull up. Place on a baking sheet with a shiny surface and bake for 12 minutes.

Yields: 4 dozen

Okra Gumbo

3 medium onions, diced
1 stalk of celery, diced
3 medium carrots, diced
1/2 cup green lima beans
1/4 cup whole kernel corn
2 large cans tomatoes, diced
3 quarts of water

2 small cans tomato paste
1 lb. okra, sliced (fresh or frozen)
1 Tbsp. gumbo filé powder
1 Tbsp. cumin

Place all ingredients, excluding okra, in soup kettle. Cook until tender. After vegetables are tender, add okra and cook until tender. Do not over cook. Season to taste with salt and freshly ground pepper. Serve over cooked white rice.

Serves 16-18

She Crab Soup

1/2 cup butter	2 Tbsp. sherry
3 cups milk	2 tsp. salt
4 cups heavy cream	Cayenne pepper
1 lb. crabmeat , picked free of all shells and cartilage	2 cups of crab roe

Melt butter in a heavy saucepan over low heat. When butter is melted, slowly stir in milk so that it is well mixed. Leave milk on low burner and cook for 20 minutes. Stir the milk frequently to keep from burning: don't let it boil.

Pour the cream into a large pot. Cook briskly for 15 minutes, until cream is thick. Pour cream into the butter and milk mixture and stir well. Add crabmeat, cook for 30 minutes to let the flavor develop.

Season soup with sherry, salt and a good sprinkle of cayenne. Add the crab roe and check for seasoning. Serve hot.

Serves 8-10

Spoon Bread

1 cup whole kernel corn	3/4 cup white
2 1/2 cups milk	cornmeal
3 whole eggs	1 tsp. sugar
3 Tbsp. melted butter	1 tsp. salt
2 Tbsp. baking powder	

Preheat oven to 375°.

Place corn in blender. Add milk and blend long enough to liquefy. Add remaining ingredients and blend. Pour batter into buttered 1 quart loaf pan or dish.

Bake for 25 minutes, or until bread has set in the center. Serve immediately.

Serves 4

Pan-Fried Quail with Country Ham

8 quail, split and flattened
2 tsp. salt
1/2 tsp. black pepper
1 tsp. dried thyme

1/2 cup unsalted butter
1/2 lb. Virginia ham
  cut into strips
1/2 cup white seedless
  grapes

Combine salt, pepper and thyme. Sprinkle sides of each bird with seasoning.

Melt butter in a large skillet over medium heat until it foams and begins to brown. Add quail, skin side down. Sprinkle with ham, cover and cook for 5 minutes until skin is golden brown. Turn the bird and continue cooking covered, until the juices run clear, about 4 minutes longer. Remove pan from heat, cover and let stand for about 10 minutes. Arrange the quail on platter, sprinkle the ham from pan over them.

Pour fat from the pan. Add grapes, 1/3 cup of water, and bring to a boil. Cook for 1 minute scraping the brown bits from bottom to deglaze the pan. Pour over quail and serve.

Serves 4

Hoppin' John

Basket Weavers
Charleston, South Carolina

1 cup dried field peas
4 cups water
2 tsp. salt

1 medium onion,
   chopped
1/2 lb. smoked jowls
1 cup raw rice

Boil peas , salt, onion and jowls in 4 cups of water until tender. In a heavy kettle, place the peas, jowls and 1 cup of the liquid from the peas with the rice and cook until the rice is done.
Serves 8

Huguenot Torte

4 eggs
3 cups sugar
8 tbsp. flour
5 tsp. baking powder
1/2 tsp. salt

2 tsp. vanilla
2 cups tart apples
   chopped
2 cups pecans,
   chopped

Preheat oven to 325°.
Beat whole eggs and sugar in electric mixer until very frothy and lemon colored. Add other ingredients and mix. Pour into two (2) well greased baking pans 8" x 12". Bake for about 45 minutes until crusty and brown.
To serve, scoop up with a pancake turner, keeping crusty part on top, garnish with whipped cream and nuts.
Serves 16

MOULTRIE TAVERN
1862

The city of Charleston with Castle Pinckney, center and Fort Sumter on the right. January 1861

Wouldn't you love to go back in time? Well, the Moultrie Tavern captures the flavor of 1862! Just off Bay Street on Vendue Range, Moultrie is an eatery and tavern representative of the mid 1800's. Period music, victuals (that's old time language for food), spirits and relics prevail here! Furnishings and prints of the Civil War are all true to the period. Waiters wear the costume of the day, and owner Robert Bohrn, who is a member of the "Palmetto brigade," wears a Confederate uniform!

Bohrn is the chef/historian/creator of Moultrie Tavern with a decidedly archaeological bent. An avid collector of civil war artifacts, he has literally shaped a museum. Bullets, bottles, muskets, buckles, children's toys, uniforms, guns, inkwells, swords and even privy pots are everywhere. What a perfect setting for the Moultrie Tavern, a place where history stands still in 1862!

The circa 1833 building was the first step in authenticity. While a large stone fireplace warms the room why not let a real mint julep or a hot cider toddy warm your innards? The purpose was to keep everything authentic and represent the plantation fare of the period. Moultrie only serves foods that were grown locally and in season in 1862. No kiwi fruit here! Venerable ales are poured such as Harp's Lager, Samuel Adams and Guiness Stout, each with a history spanning centuries of satisfying thirst.

Lighted only by candles, you'll easily feel settled into another time. Step inside a tavern and life is personal. The word tavern means hospitality in an unhurried setting. In times past, a tavern was a quiet place to retreat, eat, drink and meet with people and talk about the events of the day. In 1862, Abraham Lincoln was President. The War Between the States was going on although Charlestonians called it the "War of Northern Aggression."

Charleston was the cradle of succession. Would you like to experience the atmosphere of a camp and relive real battles? March through June sees Civil War Reinactors present Civil War Days at Fort Sumter and Fort Moultrie.

Modern day journalists have taken this tavern to heart. *USA Today, The Boston Globe* and *Fodors Travel Guide* have been entranced by this period piece. All this ambiance of another time has clearly created a distinct dining experience. And the food! Flounder Stuffed With Crabmeat and a pleasing Chicken Pie are from the luncheon menu. With each meal, great corn bread and relish trays come to the table. When you "supp" at the tavern, you're assured plain good eating with an appetizer of James Island Sautéed Shrimp with Rice. This is a great recipe! Game Pie and Leg of Lamb are typical of the menu's authenticity. Hearty appetites relish the Roast Pork with Cranberry and Apple Cider Sauce. You'll likely give out a Rebel Yell when you savor the Confederate Bean Soup. Even if you aren't a Southerner, you'll surrender to the charm of the Moultrie Tavern!

Confederate Bean Soup

1 cup onion, chopped	1/2 quart ham stock
1 cup celery, chopped	2/3 cup brown sugar
1 cup bacon, chopped	1 quart can of baked
1-3 cups Hillshire Farms	beans
sausage, sliced	1 quart heavy cream

Sauté the onion, celery and bacon in a heavy skillet. When the onion is translucent, pour off all bacon fat. Pour all the ingredients into a soup kettle, stir frequently and bring mixture to a boil and serve.

THE REISSUE OF

FRANK LESLIE'S
ILLUSTRATED
NEWS-PAPER

Entered according to the Act of Congress, in the year 1860, by FRANK LESLIE, in the Clerk's Office of the District Court for the Southern District of New York

No. 270—Vol. XI.]   NEW YORK, JANUARY 26, 1861.   [PRICE 6 CENTS.

NOTICE TO OUR READERS.

Our Special Artist in Charleston.

We are receiving every day from our Special Artist in Charleston, S. C., important and striking sketches of all the exciting events which occur in that city, its harbor and surroundings. No other representative artist from the North is or has been in Charleston during the stirring time, so the public will bear in mind that FRANK LESLIE'S ILLUSTRATED NEWSPAPER will contain the only authentic Illustrations of the Secession Movement and the important and thrilling events which arise out of it.

All pictures, therefore, in other papers, pretending to illustrate events transpiring in Charleston, are necessarily, and must be pronounced, BOGUS.

We make this statement unwillingly, but we think it right to claim whatever merit or advantage may be derived as the fruits of our enterprise, and of that conservative position which opens the way for our artists in every section of the country.

RAISING THE STARS AND STRIPES AT FORT SUMPTER.

Our artist in Charleston has furnished us with a graphic sketch of one of those incidents which throw a romantic light upon the stern face of war. A Baltimore gentleman who was also present furnishes the following account of this emphatic scene:

"It is known that the American flag brought away from Fort Moultrie was raised at Sumpter precisely at noon on the 27th ult., but the incidents of that 'flag raising' have not been re-

IMPRESSIVE SCENE AT FORT SUMPTER, ON DEC. 27, 1860, WHEN THE STARS AND STRIPES WERE RAISED—THE CHAPLAIN INVOKING A BLESSING WHILE MAJOR ANDERSON WAS HOISTING THE STANDARD.

Roast Pork with Cranberry and Apple Cider Glaze

4 to 5 lbs. boneless
loin roast
1 tsp. salt

1/2 tsp. pepper
1 package fresh
cranberries
2 cups apple cider

Season roast with salt and pepper and place on rack in an open roasting pan. Roast uncovered in moderate oven (350°) 35 minutes per lb., or to an internal temperature of 185°. In a large saucepan, combine the cranberries and cider and bring to a boil. Lower the heat and cook until all the cranberries have burst open. Allow the glaze to cool. When the meat is almost done, remove the roast from the pan and drain all the fat. Return the roast to the pan and spoon the glaze over the roast and finish baking.
Serves 6-8

James Island Sautéed Shrimp with Rice

5 shrimp, peeled
1/4 cup mushrooms, sliced
1 Tbsp. shallots, chopped
1/4 cup white wine

1/4 cup cream
Salt & pepper to taste
Fresh dill, chopped
1 cup white rice,
cooked

Sauté the shrimp and mushrooms until the shrimp turn pink. Add shallots, wine and cream. Add salt and pepper and fresh dill to taste. Stirring frequently, bring mixture to a boil and remove immediately from heat. Serve over white rice. Serves 1

Hot Cider Toddy

3/4 cup hot apple cider   1 pinch ground ginger
1 oz. bourbon (optional)   1 cinnamon stick
1 pinch ground cinnamon

Pour the hot cider into a mug then add the remaining ingredients and stir with a cinnamon stick.

Mint Julep

1 tsp. powdered sugar   2 1/2 oz. Kentucky
2 tsp. water   bourbon
Shaved ice   4 sprigs of mint

Into a silver mug put: the sugar and water and muddle (stir). Add the shaved ice and bourbon and stir gently until the mug is frosted. Insert sprigs of mint on top and serve.

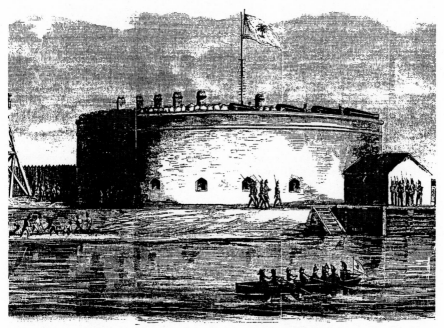

CASTLE PINCKNEY, CHARLESTON HARBOR

Pinckney Cafe

Tia Sillers-Purcell

Set in a sunny yellow frame nineteenth century house on a skinny little lot, the Pinckney Cafe is both casual and inexpensive. The character of the house is delightful. Everyone loves the comfort of an old Charleston home and Pinckney's is as cozy as my Aunt Alma Genevieve's place.

112

From the historic Market, walk up Anson Street and go past two of the carriage stables. You can look right in on the horses! At the corner, Hoppin' John has his serendipitious bookstore all about food. Hang a right at Pinckney and you'll be looking down this quaint street to the Pinckney Cafe. The horse-drawn carriages go climpity clop the wrong way on this one-way street. Ruth and Scott Fales tend their herb garden out front and live upstairs over the cafe. From a red barn nearby, a pair of skitterish hens cross the road to lay eggs on their lower step. Ruth says a small goat often walks over to trim the grass by the garden's edge. Didn't I tell you Charleston offers variety?

This is a Charleston single-house with the front door opening right onto the city sidewalk. It is just one room wide and three rooms deep. The architectural design is typical of many an English house, but it is original to Charleston with the addition of two levels of porches. They run along the side of the house rather than the front; and they are called piazzas, not porches by Charlestonians! All this was a Barbadoes influenced design to cool down the semi-tropical temperatures! The romantic result has been compared to a ship at full sail with all the canvases trimmed out to catch the ocean winds coming in from the harbor.

On a bright Spring day or a sultry southern night, dining out on the piazza is a favorite way to enjoy Pinckney style. Lunch brings soups, salads, sandwiches, a great gumbo and espresso. A pleasing Pinckney Pasta, Pan Seared Grouper with Mussels, and Carolina Jewels are the most requested dinner entrees. *Vogue* featured their Kahlua Pie! Read over my favorite recipes and you'll have a feeling for the varied Lowcountry specialities these Johnson & Wales Culinary School grads put forth! Then put on your walking shoes and head on over to this favorite eatery with "the locals."

and Espresso

113

Carolina Jewels

1/2 stick butter
1 medium onion, chopped
1/2 cup tasso, diced
4 cups baby lima beans
   fresh or frozen
Salt & pepper

2 cups tomatoes,
   peeled, seeded and
   chopped
2 cups chicken stock
2 tsp. fresh thyme or
   1 tsp. dried
6 cups grits, cooked

Melt butter in heavy skillet over low flame. Bring up 'temperature and sauté onions until translucent. Add Tasso and sauté for 2 minutes. Add remaining ingredients and simmer for 20 -30 minutes or until done. Serve over stone ground grits. Serves 4-6

Pinckney's Pasta

1/2 stick butter
Flour to dust seafood
1/2 lb shrimp, peeled and
   deveined
1/2 lb. sea scallops
4 tsp. capers
2 tsp. fresh sage,chopped

2 tsp.Italian
   parsley, chopped
1 cup seafood stock
1 1/2 lb. ravioli*
   cooked
Parmesan cheese,
   grated

Melt butter in large sauté pan over medium high flame until it begins to brown (but not burn). Add lightly floured shrimp & scallops and sauté 2 minutes on each side. Add capers, sage & parsley and sauté 1 minute. Add seafood stock and simmer 1 minute. If too thin swirl in a little more butter to thicken. Add cooked ravioli. Toss and top with fresh Parmesan cheese.
  *Prepared stuffed ravioli can be purchased from the specialty foods department at your local grocery. Serves 4

Pan Seared Grouper & Mussels
in a Saffron & Sun-dried Tomato Broth

Broth:

1/2 cup sun-dried tomatoes, plumped and chopped	1/2 tsp. each lemon & orange zest
1/2 cup roasted garlic, chopped	2 tsp. fresh thyme, chopped or 1 tsp. dried
2 cups seafood stock	1 bay leaf
1/2 tsp. saffron	Salt & pepper

Preheat the oven to 450°.

Add the sun-dried tomatoes to a little hot seafood stock to plump and soften them and set aside. Put 1/2 cup of peeled whole garlic cloves in a baking dish and sprinkle with olive oil. Roast the garlic in the oven for 20-30 minutes, turning the cloves every 5 minutes. After the cloves have cooled, chop them.

To the seafood stock, add the sun-dried tomatoes, garlic, saffron, lemon & orange zest, thyme, bay leaf, salt and freshly ground pepper. Bring up to a boil and let simmer for 15-20 minutes.

Grouper:

4 Tbsp. olive oil	6-6 oz. grouper filets
Flour for dusting fish	24 mussels (4 per serving)

Heat olive oil in large iron skillet. Dust grouper filets with flour and sear off on both sides. Pour the sun-dried tomato & saffron broth over the fish and add the mussels. Cover and cook on medium heat for 5-8 minutes.

Serves 4

Poogan's Porch

Poogan's Porch is in a white frame Charleston home built in 1888. An iron fence surrounds the tiny yard and vines of wisteria climb to an upstairs porch that gazes down a gas-lighted street. The dining rooms of this tall Victorian relic greet you in wintertime with their flickering fireplaces. Come Springtime, the back porch overlooking Gibbs Art Gallery and sunny patio dining are inviting.

Everyone asks "What is Poogan's porch?" says owner Bobby Ball. She's quick to tell you it was not the site of the first slave rebellion. (Charleston never had one.) No, it's not where Ma Poogan's cow tipped a lantern starting the "Great Fire." (That happened in Chicago and her name wasn't Poogan.) And no, it's not the platform from which fiery patriotic orators urged independence, secession or anything else for that matter!

The "Legend of Poogan" began in 1976, when the former owners left their Benji-mix dog "Poogan" behind. Poogan claimed the porch from which he could visit with passersby on Queen Street. He supervised the conversion to restaurant and took to the role of greeting guests with aplomb. Poogan's is named for this beloved canine and he is buried in the front yard with his own tombstone.

The story seems typical of the comfortable hospitality of Poogan's. It is a popular retreat at lunchtime, being on Queen Street and only moderately expensive. The dinner menu offers a mix of Lowcountry dishes, favorite cuts of beef, and waist-watcher salad plates geared downward in both cost and calories.

Great recipes! The Red Snapper with Lowcountry Sauce is easy to prepare and delicious. *Bon Appétit* featured the Bread Pudding. The Cajun Duck says company's coming and the Beer Bread uses beer to make it rise! Paul Newman came to dinner and took a loaf home. My son Reed whips up his own when I don't make it! It's *soooo* easy; just open a beer and leave out overnight. You're sure to please your favorite sportsman.

Cajun Duck

1- 5 to 7 lb. duck
2 tsp. cayenne pepper
1 Tbsp. fresh garlic,
  chopped
1 tsp. salt
1 tsp. white pepper
1 cup shallots,
  chopped

6 small dry red
  chili peppers
2 tsp. scallions,
  chopped
1/4 cup soy sauce
6 cups of rice or
  grits, cooked

Debone duck by first cutting backbone to expose rib cage. Then cut along the rib cage to release the breast meat and discard any remains from deboning. Rub the duck breast portion with a blend of cayenne pepper, garlic, salt and white pepper. Place the duck in a covered container and refrigerate overnight.

To a 3 quart stockpot, add 1/2 inch of water, the chopped shallots and marinated duck. Let simmer on low heat for 30-45 minutes. Remove the duck from the stockpot and let it cool. Do not discard stock from the pot.

Peel and discard the skin from the breast and leg portions of the duck. Chop breast and leg meat into bite size pieces. Place in saucepan along with 1/4 cup stock and simmer for 7 minutes. Drain off the excess stock. Add dry red chili peppers, scallions and soy sauce. Simmer on low heat for 2-3 minutes until peppers are soft. Remove from heat and serve over rice or grits.

Serves 4-6

Lowcountry Sauce

1 lb. white crabmeat
1 lb. small shrimp,
  shelled and deveined

1 lb. scallops,
  chopped

Place above ingredients in 1 1/2 quarts of lightly salted water. Bring water to a boil and cook for 4 minutes.

1 medium onion,
  chopped
1 small celery heart,
  chopped

2 medium bell
  peppers, chopped
1/4 lb. butter
3 Tbsp. tomato paste

Sauté the onion, celery, and bell peppers in butter. Add this to crab, shrimp and scallop mixture. Add tomato paste and let simmer.

This sauce is excellent over baked or grilled fish.

Serves 8-12

Poogan's Beer Bread

3 cups self-rising flour
3 Tbsp. sugar
1-12 oz. bottle of beer

Butter
1 egg yolk

Open the beer and let it sit overnight. Combine the flour, sugar and beer and mix well. Butter a loaf pan and preheat the oven to 375°. Bake the bread for 40 minutes, then brush the top with egg yolk and bake for an additional 5 minutes.

Yield: one loaf

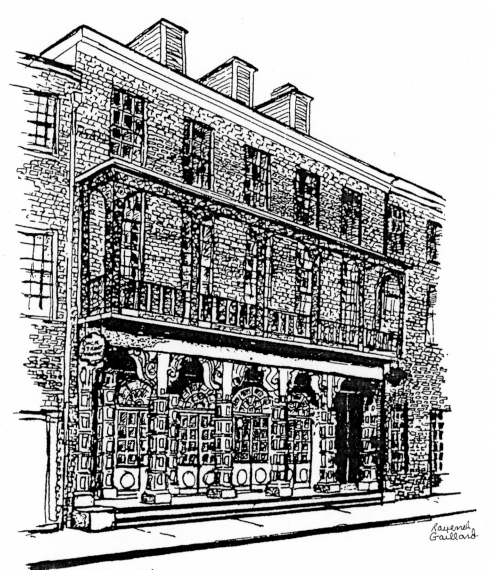

Dock Street Theater

Bread Pudding

1 loaf day old bread	2 1/2 cups sugar
1 cup raisins	4 eggs
1 Tbsp. cinnamon	1 cap yellow food
1 Tbsp. nutmeg	coloring
1 1/2 sticks of butter melted	1 quart of milk

1. Break bread into small pieces and put in a square pan. Mix in the raisins, cinnamon, nutmeg and melted butter.

2. In a medium bowl place the sugar, eggs, and food coloring while mixing well.

3. In a saucepan, heat the milk, not quite to boiling, and pour the milk into the bowl with the sugar, eggs, etc. and stir.

4. Pour the milk mixture over the bread pieces in the square pan. Let set for 5 minutes or until the bread soaks up the milk.

5. Cover the square pan with aluminum foil and bake at 350° for 30 minutes. Remove the foil and continue baking for another 30 minutes. Let pudding cool for 30 minutes then top each serving with a tablespoon of bourbon sauce.

Serves 10

Bourbon Sauce:

2 eggs	1 lb. butter, melted
1 cup powdered sugar	Bourbon to taste

Beat the eggs and sugar together in a bowl. Pour in the melted butter, add the bourbon, stir and serve.

Out Highway 53, sitting right on Shem Creek is Ronnie's. With a cypress wood interior, it has an atmosphere that is warm and bright and welcoming. It's such an escape! You can walk right out onto the docks at Shem Creek and see the shrimp boats.

Every year on May 24th, Mount Pleasant hosts The Blessing of the Fleet. This is a big event as the whole fleet of trawling boats are blessed. These romantic old boats use a trawl net to catch shrimp. The whole family enjoys this day with live entertainment, shrimp eating contests, arts and crafts and the famous parade of boats.

In this setting, it's only natural that seafood be the speciality. But premium cuts of beef, N.Y. Strip and filet mignon are showcased in the entry as well as is the wine collection. The Seafood Chowder is a great hearty recipe and just a sampling of the appetizers. The Ginger Chicken and Shrimp recipe is a runaway favorite with its tantalizing but fresh combination of flavors. It's a great make-ahead dish. It only improves sitting in the refrigerator letting the flavors mingle. And the Shrimp Creole I've made repeatedly at the request of my family.

You cannot escape the enchantment of the marshlands. Just outside the door lays an invitation to discover an ecological paradise. The stretches of quiet marsh are a subtle blend of soft gold, yellow, brown, rust and a hundred shades of green. As the tide comes in, all these colors blend into the multihued blues of the waters. This is an ever changing study of nature just teeming with life. Feel the wind. Smell that salt sea air. To enjoy it all, Ronnie's is just a natural.

Seafood Chowder

1 medium onion
2 medium carrots
4 stalks of celery
2 medium potatoes,
(all diced large)
1 tsp. dill
1 Tbsp. garlic, minced
5 Tbsp. olive oil

1 pint heavy cream
1 pint seafood stock
1 lb. shrimp, peeled
1 lb. scallops
1 lb. fish of your choice
Salt and pepper to taste
Green onions, chopped

1. In a large skillet, sauté onions, carrots, celery, potatoes, dill and garlic in olive oil over medium heat until onions become transparent and begin to simmer.

2. Add heavy cream and seafood stock. Let simmer approximately 30 minutes at a soft boil. Soup will reduce slightly, then add the shrimp, scallops and fish and let simmer for 15 minutes more. Serve with chopped green onion on top.

Yield: 1 quart

Ginger Chicken and Shrimp

1/4 cup olive oil
4 oz. chicken breast,
thinly sliced
12 medium shrimp,
peeled
1 small onion,
thinly sliced
1 small green pepper,
cut into thin strips
1 small red pepper,
cut into thin strips
1 small yellow pepper,
cut into thin strips

1 cup broccoli florettes
1 medium carrot, cut
into thin strips
1 medium yellow squash
cut into thin strips
3 Tbsp. fresh ginger
root, chopped
1 cup Teriyaki sauce
1 tsp. dijon mustard
2 cloves garlic, minced
2 cups white rice, cooked

In a large skillet heat 2 Tbsp. of the olive oil and sauté the chicken and shrimp until almost cooked. Then add all of the vegetables and cook until color changes to bright but vegetables are still crisp to the bite. Add chopped ginger, teriyaki, dijon mustard, olive oil and garlic and let simmer for approximately 5 minutes. Serve over white rice.

Serves 2

Shrimp Creole

4 Tbsp. olive oil	1 tsp. dried oregano
2 large onions, diced	1 tsp. dried basil
4 large green peppers, diced	1 Tbsp. old Bay Seasoning
1 Tbsp. garlic, minced	2 cups shrimp stock
2 cups whole peeled tomatoes crushed (canned)	20 shrimp, medium sized, peeled and deveined
	Salt & pepper to taste
2 cups tomato puree	3 cups white rice, cooked

1. In a large skillet heat 3 tablespoons of olive oil, add onions and green peppers and sauté until the onions become transparent. Add the garlic, crushed tomatoes, tomato puree, oregano, basil, Old Bay Seasoning and shrimp stock. Bring to a boil, reduce and simmer for 20 minutes.

2. In a medium skillet, heat 1 tablespoon olive oil, add shrimp and cook until bright pink in color and firm to the touch. Add cooked shrimp to creole sauce, salt and pepper to taste and serve over white rice.

Serves 4

S·A·R·A·C·E·N

It's Casablanca! You know the story. Some Moroccan Bedouin has journeyed from Tunisia to Marrakesh through narrow winding streets to this exotic place.

Saracen bids you welcome to the singularly most outrageous, one-of-a-kind, packed with sheer drama, startling architectural treasure in Charleston! Surely there is a mysterious passageway leading to an underground pit where Indiana Jones is held captive.

Moorish, Persian, Gothic and Hindu styles became a fanciful play toy for architect Francis D. Lee. Designed as the Farmers Exchange Bank in 1854, Lee was inspired

126

by England's Brighton Pavillion which set the precedent by combining these styles together. (They were inspired by The Alcazar in Seville!) The English, ever quick to coin a word, anointed this eclectic combination, Saracen. Charleston has the only example of this architecture in America.

The Moorish influence is powerfully felt in the 29 foot soaring ceiling. The upper walls and dome are painted midnight blue creating an evening sky studded with large sculpted gold-leaf stars. This arresting drama encircles the jewel-like stained glass skylight. It has all the boldness, color and magic of Van Gogh's "Starry Night."

Years of abandonment culmininated in a date with the wrecking bar, all to make way for a parking lot. Then Senator Hollings utilized it for an office in the sixties. And Horror! It was converted into a two story.

Enter swashbuckling Charlie Farrell on the scene, reclaiming the entire height; restoring the former glory of Saracen. She heard the music of "Sherharazade." She saw the perfect setting for her "nuit de mystere," a grand masked ball that was to come. She envisioned a feast that exposed people to food not available anywhere else. She was a woman with a mission.

Our heroine set her drama against this multicolored interior with frescoes and rosette windows beneath towering Arabic arches. She chose Spanish/Moorish chairs covered in a rich tapestry with the look of a Serapi rug to provide seating in this theater for food.

And Charlie delivers the culinary counterpart to this unforgettable architecture! She is the chef/founder/creator; a virtual one-woman renaissance. Her food preparation too, is eclectic, as ever-changing as the seasons and loosely described as International. Charlie's cooked for years. She likes light sauces, and has a deft touch with seasonings and herbs producing wonderful taste sensations for her exceptional dinners served Monday through Saturday.

A quote on the menu: "The discovery of a new dish does more for the happiness of mankind than the discovery of a star," confirmed for me this was my kind of place. Oysters cooked with thyme. Heavenly. An appetizer of Mussels in a Ragout of Fennel, Saffron, Cream and Pernod with Toasted Brioch reached out to tempt me. The entrees flooded my senses with a Mint Roasted Rack of Lamb, Grilled Thai Chicken and Ginger Sausage smothered in a Spicy Peanut-Coconut Sauce and a killer Morocan Barbeque Almond Duck. Sorcerer's choice: dessert of Chocolate Soufflé.

Abandon the twentieth century. Come to Casablanca. Sense an extra whiff of an exotic fragrant perfume, breathe deep. You're a smoldering Ingrid Bergman walking into this setting. Bogart's upstairs leaning against the bar. It's Marrakesh, and it's a feast day.

Dateline: December 1994. Saracen temporarily closed for Hollywood's latest filming here. Substitute Bucharest for Merrakesh; Bruce Willis for Bogart; and Die Hard III for Casablanca. But I'm still humming, "As Time Goes By."

Oysters with Thyme

2 to 3 Tbsp. butter	1/2 tsp. Tabasco sauce
2 shallots, minced	1 1/2 cups cream
1 stalk celery, minced	1/4 cup white wine
Pinch of cayenne pepper	48 oysters
1 1/2 Tbsp. fresh thyme, minced	Salt and pepper
	Toast points

Melt butter and sauté shallots and celery for 1 minute. Add cayenne and sauté 1 minute longer. Add Tabasco, thyme, cream and wine; reduce sauce until slightly thickened, stirring as needed. Add oysters and simmer in sauce approximately 2 minutes, until just cooked through. Season with salt and pepper and serve over toast points.

Serves 4 to 6

Lemon Linguine

with Fresh Shrimp, Scallops, Tomato Julienne, Mustard Greens and Tarragon in a Sherry Cream Sauce

12 oz. fresh lemon linguine or other pasta	1 1/2 cups heavy cream
	Salt and pepper to taste
10 oz. fresh shrimp, peeled & deveined	2 plum tomatoes, peeled, seeded and cut into strips
10 oz. fresh sea scallops with muscle removed	1 1/2 Tbsp. fresh tarragon, chopped
2 Tbsp. olive oil	1 cup mustard greens, cut into thin strips
2 Tbsp. sherry vinegar	

Bring a large pot of water to a rolling boil and add 1 tablespoon of salt. Heat olive oil in a large sauté pan. When very hot add shrimp and scallops and sear on either side, remove shrimp and scallops to a plate and keep warm. Return pan to heat and deglaze with sherry vinegar stirring up any bits stuck to the pan. Add the cream and bring to a boil, let reduce for 3 minutes. While cream is reducing plunge linguine into boiling water and bring water back to a boil and cook for 3-5 minutes until al denté. Drain. Add Shrimp and scallops to cream along with salt and pepper, tomato julienne and tarragon and heat through. Add linguine and mustard greens and toss thoroughly. Adjust seasoning to taste.

Serves 4

Parmesan Pudding

2 cups cream
6 large egg yolks
1 cup Parmesan cheese,
  freshly grated

1 cup bread crumbs
Salt, cayenne pepper
  and nutmeg to taste
Butter

Preheat oven to 325°.

Mix all ingredients together except the butter. Generously butter 6 custard cups. Fill cups 3/4 full and bake for 25 to 30 minutes or until golden brown. Cool for 5 minutes and unmold. Serve hot with blanched, fresh asparagus, balsamic vinegar and fresh Parmesan shavings.

Serves 6

The View from the Garden
The Battery Carriage House Inn
Charleston, SC

"The discovery of a new dish does more for the happiness of mankind than the discovery of a star"
Brillat-Savarin

Hot Chocolate Soufflé

100 grams semi-sweet or
   bitter-sweet chocolate
120 grams unsalted butter
100 ml. heavy cream
50 grams unsweetened
   cocoa powder

5 eggs, separated
45 grams sugar
8 chuncks of chocolate
Unslated butter, softened
Sugar

Preheat oven to 400°.

Butter 8 ovenproof ramekins using upward strokes, refridgerate and when cold repeat the process one more time. Dust with sugar and remove any excess butter and sugar by running thumb around top rim of ramekin. Over hot water melt chocolate and butter together. Warm cream over a low heat. When chocolate and butter are completely melted, stir to blend and add cream, cocoa and egg yolks. Stir to blend and keep warm over the warm water, but don't let it "cook". Beat egg whites until they form soft peaks and while continuing to beat, slowly add sugar and beat until firm but not dry. Remove chocolate mixture from heat and fold in 1/3 of egg whites and then quickly but gently fold chocolate mixture into rest of egg whites. Pour into prepared ramekins and drop a chunk of chocolate into each ramekin. Again run thumb around top edge of ramekin to clean any spills. Bake for 8 minutes.

Serves 8

St. Andrew's Parish Church

On Ashley River Road, sheltered among a grove of live oaks, all festooned with Spanish moss, lies Saint Andrews Parish Episcopal Church. This is the road to both Magnolia and Middleton Gardens, Drayton Hall, Millbrook Plantation and Runnymede, to name just a few. The Tearoom at St. Andrews makes a delightful place to stop, relax, and enjoy a pleasant lunch in the spring.

Being the oldest church building in South Carolina, it is one of the very few Colonial churches with this form of architecture. The timbers and nails were made on the grounds. It borders its own swamp of cypress, and by the roadside is an ancient graveyard with tombstones that make excellent reading and tell their own tale of the lives and times of parishes past.

Saint Andrews was one of the wealthiest parishes in the colonies and much of the wealth was derived from indigo, used as a dye. When the crop declined, the parish dwindled. When Reverend John Grimke-Drayton died in 1891, there were few members that remained in the church. Reverend Drayton is largely responsible for the beauty of Magnolia Gardens, having planted the many azaleas and camellias that grace the grounds.

Today St. Andrews is a thriving parish. The women of the church are to be commended for their work as they both stock a gift shop and open the Tea Room. Although open only mid-March through mid-April, hundreds of people a day are served. Fresh flowers are on every table and the waitresses wear colonial costume. This is a popular place to stop on your way to or from the gardens.

The Lowcountry menu features a terrific Okra Soup and Shrimp Paste sandwiches. Shrimp paste is traditionally made into a mold and served for breakfast. Today it is more often served with benne wafers or toast squares as an accompaniment for drinks.

The rich toothsome desserts of the south have always seemed irreconcilable to the seventeen-inch waistlines claimed by the ladies. But there they were: Tipsy Pudding bursting with whipping cream, sugar, eggs and sherry;

Plantation Pecan Pie with brown sugar, syrup and eggs; pecan muffins, and a heaven-sent Magnolia Pie that they always run out of!

Saint Andrews' little cookbook gives a charming poem (by someone named anonymous!) and it reads like this:

Ye've left the lovely Southern manse
With its tree-lined, flowered broad expanse.
Thine eyes are filled, now fill thy mouth
With delectable morsels from the South.

Pecan Muffins

2 eggs, beaten
1 cup brown sugar, packed
1/3 cup butter, melted

1/2 cup self-rising flour
1 tsp. vanilla
1/2 to 1 cup pecans
Baking cups

Mix all ingredients together. Pour into baking cups. Bake at 350° for 25 minutes.

Yield: 1 dozen

Shrimp Paste

Shrimp, boiled, shelled and deveined
Mayonnaise
Salt & pepper

Worcestershire
Pinch of mace
Sherry (optional)

Grind the shrimp or chop as fine as possible and pound them into a paste. In a large mixing bowl combine the mayonnaise, salt, pepper and Worcestershire sauce to taste. When thoroughly mixed add the mace and shrimp, and beat until smooth. Chill for several hours before serving.

To Boil Crabs

Bring water to a boil. Throw in the live crabs. Boil 30 minutes.

To Boil Shrimp

Wash thoroughly. Boil 4 to 5 minutes in enough salted water to cover them. Cool. Peel.

To Fry Shrimp

Shell and clean vein from back. It is convenient to leave tails on. They look prettier, too. Salt. Prepare 3 small bowls: one with flour, one with beaten egg and milk and one with cracker meal. Dip each shrimp in the mixtures named above and in the order listed. When all are prepared, fry in hot deep fat; drain and serve with tartar sauce or lemon juice with melted butter. For a change, try mixing 2 tablespoons mayonnaise with 2 tablespoons catsup, a dash of Worcestershire sauce and 1 teaspoon lemon juice.

Windmills and watermills were common in the neighboring areas along the Ashley River circa 1800.

Tipsy Pudding

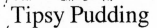

4 egg yolks	1/2 cup cold water
1 cup sugar	4 egg whites
3/4 cup sherry wine	1 pint
1 envelope gelatin	whipping cream
	1 angel food cake

Cook the egg yolks, 1/2 cup of the sugar and the sherry in the top of a double boiler until the mixture thickens. Soak the gelatine in the cold water. Whip the egg whites until small peaks form. Combine the remaining 1/2 cup of sugar with the heavy cream and whip. Add all the mixtures together and fold gently. Break an angel food cake in pieces and place it in the bottom of a large bowl. Pour the Tipsy Pudding over the cake, and chill overnight. Serves 6-8

Magnolia Pie

4 eggs	1 pkg. Knox
3 lg. pkgs. cream cheese,	unflavored gelatin
softened	2 crumb pie crusts
1 1/2 cups sugar	6 Tbsp.sugar
Juice of 2 lemons, plus	1 pint sour cream
the zest	

Beat eggs well. Beat in softened cream cheese and 1 1/2 cups sugar. Blend until smooth. Add all the zest plus the juice of <u>one</u> lemon along with the Knox gelatin while stirring. Pour into two crumb pie crusts. (You may use commercially prepared crusts.) Bake at 350° for about 30 minutes. While the pies are baking, combine the 6 tbsp. of sugar and remaining lemon juice with the sour cream. Stir as little as possible. Return mixture to refrigerator. Remove pies from oven and allow to cool slightly. Spread sour cream topping on each pie and return to oven for 5 minutes. Refrigerate overnight. Yield: 2 pies

Ashley River Mud Cake

2 sticks butter or margarine	1 tsp. baking soda
4 Tbsp. cocoa	1/2 tsp. salt
1 cup water	1/2 cup buttermilk
2 cups sugar	2 eggs
2 cups flour	1 tsp. vanilla

Melt the butter or margarine and add the cocoa and water. Bring to a boil. Mix the sugar, flour, baking soda and salt together in a medium bowl. Add the chocolate mixture and stir with a wire whisk. Add buttermilk, eggs and vanilla. Mix well and pour into greased jelly roll pan. Bake at 350° for 20 minutes.

Icing:

1 stick butter or margarine	1 box 4 X sugar
4 Tbsp. cocoa	1/2 cup nuts
6 Tbsp. buttermilk	1 tbsp. vanilla

Make the icing while the cake bakes. Melt the butter or margarine and add the cocoa and buttermilk. Bring to a boil and add the remaining ingredients.while stirring. Put icing on cake while still warm. You can make, bake, frost and have the cake ready to eat in less than an hour.

Yield: 1 cake

Tucked away on Church Street, just off the market is a true Irish pub and restaurant. Step into Tommy Condon's for a bit of frolic, laughter and song for the whole family. The pub is softened with brown wainscotting and is a faithful duplication of a pub from the ol' country. The warm ambiance will lift your spirits with a light hearted respite. Tommy took many trips to Ireland to get it down right, scouring pub mirrors from all around the Irish countryside, and striking a bargain with both Gypsy and tinker. Often asked why an Irish pub in Charleston, Tommy replies good naturedly "Scarlet was Irish!"

An Emerald Isle welcome offers a tot of Guinness,

a pint of Bushmills or a draft of Killian's Irish Red. This is a family place where all the generations are welcome and the children have a menu for "little Leprechauns."

Hearty Irish fare is exemplified in the bountiful Shepherd's Pie. My whole family orders this one rousing dish! Ample servings provide satisfaction. This is soul food for anyone of Brit or Irish descent! Be sure to try the Irish Potato Chowder. It is a 19th century Condon family recipe brought over from the old sod. If you suspect the potato of being sacred to the Irish, you're right, the Irish came to America in droves after the great potato famine! Seafood and Lowcountry items are offered as well. Varied menu selections include a mighty fine Donegal Chicken Pie, Corned Beef of course and a Tipperary Sirloin. Also notable is the Lowcountry favorite, Shrimp and Grits. Top off the meal with Irish coffee.

Thursday to Sunday night brings the spirited sounds of Ireland for sing-alongs. A jolly combo from Dublin's Hog N' Fool played when I was last there. Everyone loves Condon's: young couples, families, boisterous groups, and grandparents all enjoy the neighborly feeling. Condon's issues a hearty welcome: Once here, everyone's Irish! This is a place for conviviality, a long winded gab in the spirit of Yeats, and the "good feed" to be had here. When you walk out of Condon's you'll vow like Scarlet, "I"m never going to be hungry again!"

Irish Coffee

1 jigger Irish whiskey
2 tsp. dark brown sugar
Chilled fresh whipped
  cream

Freshly brewed
piping
hot coffee

Heat the whiskey and sugar. Preheat the glass or cup. Dip the glass rim in the liquor before pouring in the whiskey and sugar. Fill to the top with coffee and stir. Top with whipped cream and serve immediately.
Yield: 1 cup

Shrimp and Grits

1 1/2 lb. small shrimp, peeled and deveined
1/3 cup red onion, diced
1/3 cup green pepper, chopped
1/3 cup celery, chopped
4 Tbsp. margarine
1/2 tsp. garlic, chopped
1/2 tsp. cayenne
1 tsp. Old Bay Seasoning
1 tsp. Worchestershire sauce
4 Tbsp. diced tomatoes
2 Tbsp. flour
1 cup half & half

1. In 2 quart saucepan sauté vegetables and shrimp in margarine until shrimp are firm.

2. Add garlic, cayenne pepper, Old Bay Seasoning, Worchestershire sauce, and diced tomatoes then sauté at low heat for approximately 2 minutes.

3. Add flour and stir quickly, blending in evenly.

4. Slowly add half & half until entire mixture is smooth and creamy.

5. Prepare four portions of grits in bowls. Instant or regular. Follow directions on package.

6. Pour shrimp mixture over grits and serve.

Yield: 4 portions

Shepherd's Pie

4 large potatoes, peeled and cut in half
3 Tbsp. butter
1/2 cup milk
Salt & pepper to taste

Cook the potatoes in boiling water for 15-20 minutes. Drain off the water and add butter, plus salt and freshly ground pepper. Mash the potatoes and add the milk. Continue mashing until smooth and set aside.

2 Tbsp. cooking oil
1 large onion, chopped
1 lb. ground beef
1 large carrot, grated
2 stalks celery, chopped
8 mushrooms, sliced
1/2 tsp. thyme

2 Tbsp. fresh
  parsley, chopped
2 cloves garlic,
  minced
4 oz. of Guinness
  Extra Stout
Salt & pepper

Preheat oven to 375 °.

Heat the oil in a heavy skillet and sauté the onion until transparent. Add the ground beef stirring to break up any large lumps. Add the carrot, celery, mushrooms, thyme, parsley and garlic while stirring. Sauté on medium heat for about 10 minutes, stirring to keep the meat from sticking to the skillet. Add the Guinness Extra Stout plus the salt and pepper to taste.

Spread meat and vegetable mixture in deep baking dish. Spread the mashed potatoes over the top leaving peaks in the middle. Bake for 1/2 hour or until the potatoes are nicely browned.

Keep a bottle of Worcestershire sauce on the table to add an extra zing to this delicious pie.

Serves 4

THE

TRAWLER

A beckoning lighthouse marks the entrance to the Trawler. It is all that has survived of the old original landmark. 1989 dealt a double curse with both a fire and a hurricane. The fire came first and construction was almost complete when Hugo hit. With true tenacity and fortitude, the Semper family prevailed and a Charleston tradition was saved.

The new Trawler has kept much of the character enjoyed by generations of visitors but is more open like a beach house. The Trawler takes its name from the boats that go out into the ocean dragging their nets. It is a way of life along the Carolina coast and Mount Pleasant is home base to a whole shrimping fleet. On their return trip the trawler crew pulls in their haul and removes the shrimp heads. They are ready for market by sunset when they dock at Shem creek.

Just to give you an idea of how varied the seafood selection is, there are six ways to order crab, eight for shrimp, dozens more for clams, oysters and fish. With lobster, frog legs, squid and scallops somewhere in between, and mermaid being the only thing from the sea not on the menu, the possibilities are endless. All the seafood here couldn't be fresher. It is caught daily by the boats docked on Shem Creek.

The Crab Dip is legendary! People have bought this book for the one recipe! Once you make it for your family or a party this is one that will be marked and passed around!

Just outside the Trawler are docks where deep sea fishing boats are moored. With names like *Atlantic Star*, *Thunder Star* and *Carolina Clipper* they promise balmy adventures. Further down Shem Creek you can visit a whole shrimping fleet. Breathe deep and smell that salt sea air! Around sunset those girls *Miss Diane* and *Miss Marilyn,* all festooned with nets, should be bringing their bountiful catch home.

The Trawler's
Famous Crab Dip

1 1/4 cups mayonnaise
   heavy duty,
   (restaurant type if
   possible)
1 cup crabmeat

1/2 cup cheddar
   cheese grated fine
1 tsp. horseradish
4 Tbsp. French
   dressing

Mix all of the above ingredients and serve with crackers. If you prefer a little extra tang, don't be afraid to add more horseradish or French dressing to suit your taste.

143

The Variety Store

Perched high on pilings over the water at the Municipal Yacht Basin is this surprise. The Variety Store is actually a store equipped to serve the needs of the sailors and crews of the boats anchored in the waters out its door. Need requisitions while in port? The ship's store can supply you with every provision from java, to a nautical map, to a good rope. But come dinner time, the Altine family is in charge. Taught by the former chef on Onassis's yacht, the family serves up a simple menu, all fresh and delicious and has them waiting in line.

Scallops Sautéed in Bacon

2 dozen large scallops	Paprika
2 Tbsp. butter	Parsley, chopped
2 strips bacon	Salt & pepper

Sauté scallops slowly in buttered skillet with bacon about 7-8 minutes until brown. Add paprika, parsley, salt and freshly ground pepper and serve.
Yield: 2 portions

Smoked Salmon Dip

1 can red or pink salmon	1 tsp. liquid smoke
8 ounces cream cheese	

Mix together well and serve on melba toast or crackers.

Key Lime Pie

6 egg yolks, beaten slightly	1 9-inch baked pie shell
1 can sweetened condensed milk	6 egg whites
1/2 cup lime juice	1/2 tsp. cream of tartar
	6 Tbsp. sugar

Preheat oven to 300°.
Combine egg yolks, condensed milk and lime juice. Blend well. Pour into baked pie shell. Beat egg whites until frothy. Add cream of tartar and continue to beat until stiff. Gradually add sugar and beat until meringue is stiff and glossy. Swirl onto top of pie. Bake in oven until meringue is golden brown.
Yield: 6-8 portions

VILLAGE

C · A · F · E

The Village Cafe is exactly what it sounds like, only better! It lies on tiny Mill Street, nestled on Shem Creek, in Mount Pleasant. But don't let this cottage fool you. The "little" Village Cafe is one of five South Carolina restaurants to receive the prestigious "Dirona Award" for excellence in delicious food, great wines, and service that is extraordinary.

Intimate dining rooms await you in this cozy building. Soft pastels and crisp whites are the perfect backdrop for some really lovely works of art that add color and warmth. Serving lunch, dinner, and a bountiful brunch on Sundays, the rooms are sunlit by day and at night are mellowed by soft candlelight.

But the melting pot of American culture is heating up in this kitchen. Chef Jason Ulak trained with Scott Roark, the former chef and founder of the Village Cafe. Scott is to be credited with the creation of innovative recipes and a great overall concept. The "nouvelle American cuisine" theme is enhanced by an extensive wine list of American wines from the Sonoma and Napa wineries as well as available by the glass.

The luncheon menu is light and fresh. An extensive dinner menu features exotic "starters" insisting that you choose Black Bean Crepe, Pecan-Fried Brie over assorted greens among other selections. If you're she-crabbed out try the Sweet Pepper, Roasted Corn and Blue Crab Soup. The Black Grouper "en Papillote" is a treasure of a recipe. Try this at home and top with the Red Pepper Sauce which is also a wow over grilled chicken. The Goat Cheesecake over Mesclun Greens is just outstanding and the Sundried Tomato Vinaigrette recipe is a must-have to please your family and friends! The White Chocolate Banana Cream Pie is a scrumptious dessert, homemade of course! Try these recipes and you'll understand why American food is more admired than ever. You may decide to attend their cooking school held each Spring!

Saunter on over to The Common, a cluster of shops just a stone's throw away. The Museum of the Common has a Hurricane Hugo exhibit that will make you stand in awe at the force of nature.

Goat Cheesecake

over Mesclun Greens
with a Sundried Tomato Vinaigrette

1 loaf goat cheesecake	1 1/4 cup
6 cups mesclun greens	sundried tomato
Crisp potato julienne	vinaigrette
for garnish	

Slice the goat cheesecakes into 6 slices. Toss the sundried tomato vinaigrette with the mesclun greens and garnish with the julienne potato.
    Yield: 6 portions

Goat Cheesecake:

3/4 cup crackers,	1/2 cup heavy
sesame or any flavor	cream
6 Tbsp. butter	6 eggs
1 1/2 lb. cream cheese	1 Tbsp. rosemary,
1 1/2 lb. goat cheese	chopped fine

Preheat oven to 300°
Grind the crackers into fine crumbs and mix with butter. Line the baking pan with the crumb mixture. Combine the cream and coat cheeses in mixer and whip until smooth. Scrap the sides with a rubber spatula and add the heavy cream and the eggs. Whip until smooth, then stir in rosemary. Pour batter into the lined pan and bake in a waterbath in oven for 1 hour.
    Yield: 1 loaf

Sun-dried Tomato Vinaigrette:

1/2 cup sun-dried tomatoes
1/2 Tbsp. dijon mustard
1/2 Tbsp. shallots, minced
2 Tbsp. rice vinegar
1 Tbsp. balsamic
 vinegar
1/2 tsp. thyme,
 fresh & chopped
1/2 cup olive oil
Juice from
 tomatoes
Salt & pepper

Soak sun-dried tomatoes in hot water until they are softened, then remove. In a bowl, add the dijon mustard, shallots, vinegars and thyme. Slowly add the olive oil while continuing to whisk, until the solution is emulsified. Add tomatoes and little bit of the juice from the tomatoes if the dressing becomes too thick. Season with salt and freshly ground black pepper to taste.
 Yield: 1 1/4 cups

Red Pepper Sauce

6 large red bell peppers,
 seeded & roughly
 chopped
2 shallots, chopped
1 tsp. cumin
1 tsp. chili powder
3 cups chicken
 stock or canned
 low-sodium
 chicken broth
1 Tbsp. olive oil
Salt and pepper

Heat oil in large skillet. Quickly sauté shallots; add chopped red peppers and sauté about 2 minutes or just before they become tender. Stir spices into peppers; add chicken stock. Simmer about 5 minutes. Remove from heat and puree in blender or food processor. Strain. Add salt and pepper to taste.
 This sauce is particularly good with grilled fish and smoked chicken.
 Yield: 1 quart (16 1/4-cup servings)

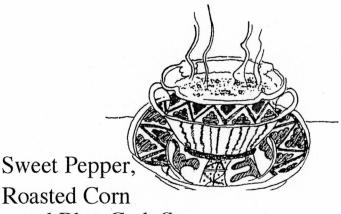

Sweet Pepper, Roasted Corn and Blue Crab Soup

8 large sweet peppers (red, yellow, green assortment) seeded and roughly chopped	1 quart chicken stock
4 ears corn, shucked and washed	1 tsp. olive oil
1 yellow onion, thinly sliced	2 Tbsp. cornstarch mixed with an equal amount of water
1 lb. blue-crab meat, lump or special, well-packed	Salt & pepper
	1 dash Tabasco sauce
	2 Tbsp. Worcestershire sauce

Preheat oven to 350°.

Place corn on a sheet pan and roast approximately 15 minutes. Remove when tender and slice from cob. Steep corn cobs in 1 quart water for 30 minutes. Remove cobs, strain and reserve stock. Set aside. Sauté the sliced onion in olive oil. Do not brown. Add peppers and cook until tender. Add chicken stock and cook about 5 minutes.

Puree the pepper and onion mixture in a food processor or blender, then strain. Put back on medium heat and add corn stock, cooked corn and bring to a simmer. Add cornstarch mixture, slowly while stirring to thicken slightly. Remove from heat. Stir in crabmeat and season to taste.

Yield: 8 portions

Black Grouper "en Papillote"

6 oz. filets of
  black grouper
3 cups lemon
  thyme broth
1/2 cup julienne carrots
1/2 cup julienne sweet
  peppers
I bunch asparagus
  (about 1 lb.)

2 cups
  quartered new
  potatoes, blanched
1 1/2 cups broccoli
  florets
6 sheets parchment
  paper
Black pepper

Preheat oven to 300°.

On the right half of each sheet of parchment paper, place a grouper filet and arrange vegetables in a pleasing array. Ladle broth over, season with freshly ground black pepper and fold parchment paper to conceal ingredients. Bake papillote in oven for 20 minutes. To serve, transfer the papillote to serving plate and slice open the top of the bag with a knife and carefully peel open the bag. (The steam is very hot.) Serve immediately. Deserves a Wow!

Yield:6 portions

Lemon Thyme Broth:

3 cups chicken broth
1/4 cup lemon
  juice, fresh
1 whole lemon zest,
  chopped fine
5 sprigs fresh thyme
2 tsp. shallots, minced

1 stalk celery,
  chopped
1/2 carrot, chopped
1/2 onion, chopped
1 bay leaf
5 white
  peppercorns

Combine all ingredients together and simmer for 25 minutes, **DO NOT BOIL!** Ready to serve.

White Chocolate Banana Cream Pie

Pie Crust:

3 parts flour
2 parts butter
1 part water

Pinch of salt
2 Tbsp. sugar

Mix all dry ingredients together. Add butter and mix until mixture gets mealy. Add water and combine just until mixture forms a ball. Remove and cover with aluminum foil and refrigerate. Line a 10" removable bottom pan with dough. Place a piece of parchment paper inside and fill with rice or dried beans. (These are used only for baking the dough.) When dough has finished baking, remove filling and parchment paper.

White Chocolate Mousse:

3 egg yolks
14 oz. white chocolate,
   melted

1/4 cup 10 X sugar
1 1/2 cup heavy
   cream

Beat yolks with sugar until light yellow in color (ribbon stage). Whip heavy cream until it reaches soft peaks. Blend 1/3 of cream with yolk mixture and add to white chocolate. Fold in the rest of the cream and blend until smooth. Refrigerate over night until ready to use.

Pastry Cream:

2 cups milk
4 oz. sugar
2 eggs
2 egg yolks

3 tbsp. cornstarch
1/4 cup vanilla
1 Tbsp. creme
   de banana

Heat milk to just before boil. Mix sugar and cornstarch together. Make a well in the center and add the eggs and the yolks and slowly incorporate until smooth. Temper hot milk with egg mixture by slowly adding and whisking at the same time until all the milk is incorporated. Return to the stove and add vanilla and cream de banana and heat over **low** heat. Continuously stir until the pastry cream thickens. If heat is too high, it will scramble the eggs so watch the cream carefully. Strain and then whisk in the butter. Refrigerate.

To Make Pie:

2 cups white chocolate mousse	1 baked pie shell
2 cups pastry cream	4 bananas
	White chocolate shavings

Spread pastry cream on bottom of pie shell. Slice bananas and layer them on top of the pastry cream. Spoon white chocolate mousse on top and garnish with white chocolate shavings. Refrigerate.

Yield: 1 pie

CHARLESTON, SOUTH CAROLINA

Page

APPETIZERS

Carolina Pea Cakes from Carolina's...................... 47
Coquilles St. Jacques from The Barbadoes Room...... 26
Crabmeat in Mushroom Caps from Marianne........... 92
Goat Cheesecake over Mesclun Greens
    from The Village Cafe....................................148
Grilled Clams with a Garlic Chive Butter
    from 82 Queen... 67
Mussels Marianne from Marianne........................ 93
Oysters Elizabeth from 82 Queen.......................... 67
Oysters with Thyme from Saracen.........................128
Parmesan Pudding from Saracen...........................129
Scallops Sautéed in Bacon from The Variety Store.....145
Shrimp Paste from St. Andrew's Tea Room...........134
Shuck's Special from A.W. Shuck's...................... 21
Skillet Seared Yellow Grits with Tasso Gravy
    from Magnolia's..84
Smoked Salmon Dip from The Variety Store............145
Spicy Shrimp and Sausage over Creamy White Grits
    with Tasso Gravy from Magnolia's..................... 82
St. Jacques Grilles Aux Asparagus from Beaumont's.. 31
The Trawler's Famous Crab Dip from The Trawler....143

BREADS

Middleton Biscuits from Middleton Place Restaurant..102
Pecan Muffins from St. Andrew's Tea Room..........134
Poogan's Beer Bread from Poogan's Porch.............119
Southern Corn Bread from Bessinger's.................. 38
Spoon Bread from Middleton Place Restaurant.........103

DESSERTS

,Ashley River Mud Cake from St. Andrew's
    Tea Room..137
Banana Foster from 82 Queen............................70
Bourbon Pecan Pie from Edgar's........................63

Bread Pudding with Bourbon Sauce from
Poogan's Porch...121
Buttermilk Tart with Fresh Raspberries
from Louis's Charleston Grill 79
Chocolate Mousse from The Barbadoes Room.........29
Cream Cheese Brownie
with Chocolate Sauce from Magnolia's...............86
Créme Brûlée from Beaumont's..........................34
Death by Chocolate from 82 Queen.....................70
Hot Chocolate Soufflé from Saracen....................131
Huguenot Torte from Middleton Place Restaurant.....105
Key Lime Pie from The Variety Store..................145
Lemon Chess Pie from Alexander's......................19
Magnolia Pie from St. Andrew's Tea Room............136
Papaya Cream Cheese Tart
with Macadamia nuts from Marianne..................94
Pastry Crust from Bessinger's...........................39
Peach Cobbler from Bessinger's.........................39
Pears in Wine from Bocci's..............................43
Strawberry Banana Pie from 82 Queen.................71
Supreme au Chocolat from Beaumont's.................35
Sweet Grits Cake Sautéed
with Seasonal Berries from Carolina's................51
Tipsy Pudding from St. Andrews Tea Room.......... 136
Toll House Pie from Alexander's.........................19
White Chocolate Banana Cream Pie
from The Village Cafe 152

EGG DISHES

Seafood Quiche from Alexander's........................17
Shrimp Fried Rice from A.W. Shuck's..................23

DRINKS

Hot Cider Toddy from Moultrie Tavern.................111
Irish Coffee from Tommy Condon's....................139
Mint Julep from Moultrie Tavern........................111

FOWL

Carolina Pigeon Stewed with Winter Vegetables
from Louis's Charleston Grill........................... 76
Cajun Duck from Poogan's Porch.......................118
Chicken Jambalaya from The East Bay
Trading Company... 59
Ginger Chicken and Shrimp from Ronnie's.............124
Lemon-Basil Chicken from Bocci's....................... 42
Pan-Fried Quail with County Ham
from Middleton Place Restaurant.......................104
Sautéed Chicken Breast
with Tarragon Sauce from Beaumont's................ 33
West Indies Chicken from The Barbadoes Room....... 27

MEATS

Carolina Jewels from The Pinckney Cafe..............114
Country Ham with Pan-Fried Quail
from Middleton Place Restaurant.......................104
Roast Pork with Cranberry and Apple Cider Glaze
from Moultrie Tavern.....................................110
Shepherd's Pie from Tommy Condon's.................141

PASTA

Angel Hair Pasta with Shrimp & Spicy Pesto
from Bocci's.. 42
Lemon Linguine with Fresh Shrimp, Scallops,
Tomato Julienne, Mustard Greens and Tarragon
in a Sherry Cream Sauce from Saracen................130
Pinckney's Pasta from The Pinckney Cafe.............114
Shrimp Alfredo from Bocci's............................ 41

SALADS & DRESSINGS

Almond Salmon over Warm Spinach Salad
from Edgar's...62
Asparagus and Wild Mushroom Salad from
82 Queen...66

Chicken Salad in a Coconut from
   The Barbadoes Room....................................28
Cole Slaw from Bessinger's............................38
Creamy Pepper Dressing from 82 Queen................66
Goat Cheesecake over Mesclun Greens with a
   Sundried Tomato Vinaigrette from the Village Cafe..148
Hot Spinach Salad from The Barbadoes Room..........28
Lemon Lingonberry Vinaigrette from Magnolia's.......85
Peanut-Raspberry Vinaigrette from Carolina's..........48
Shrimp and Cucumber Salad from Alexander's.........16
Shrimp Salad from the Charleston Crab House.........55
Sun-dried Tomato Vinaigrette from the Village Cafe..149

SAUCES

Basil Pesto from Bocci's................................43
Béchamel Sauce from Bocci's...........................41
Béchamel Sauce from Marianne.......................92
Bourbon Sauce from Poogan's Porch..................121
Chocolate Sauce from Magnolia.........................86
Curry Sauce from The Barbadoes Room................27
Lowcountry Sauce from Poogan's Porch..............119
Red Pepper Sauce from The Village Cafe..............149
Rémoulade Sauce from Carolina's.......................50
Saffron & Sun-dried Tomato Broth
   from The Pinckney Cafe..............................115
Southern Comfort BBQ Sauce from Alexander's.......16
Sweet Red Pepper Cream Sauce from 82 Queen......68
Tasso Gravy from Magnolia's...........................83

SEAFOOD

Angel Hair Pasta with Shrimp & Spicy Pesto
   from Bocci's...42
BBQ Shrimp in Southern Comfort Sauce
   from Alexander's..16
Beaufort Stew from Alexander's.......................18
Black Grouper "*en Papillote*" from the Village Cafe..151
Carolina's Crab Cakes with Rémoulade Sauce
   from Carolina's...50

Casserole of Drunken Fishes
      from The East Bay Trading Company..................58
Coquilles St. Jacques from The Barbadoes Room 26
Crabmeat in Mushroom Caps from Marianne...........92
Crawfish Tails and Crabmeat in Caviar Butter Sauce
      from Louis's Charleston Grill............................78
Deviled Crab from The Charleston Crab House.........54
Ellis Creek Casserole for One from A.W. Shuck's.....22
Fried Soft-Shell Crabs
      from The Charleston Crab House.......................55
Geeche Bowl Dinner for 4 from A.W.Shuck's..........22
Ginger Shrimp and Chicken fronm Ronnie's...........124
Grilled Clams with a Garlic Chive Butter
      from 82 Queen..67
James Island Sautéed Shrimp with Rice
      from Moultrie Tavern.....................................110
La Charlestonaisse Bouillabaisse from Marianne........91
Lemon Linguine with fresh Shrimp, Scallops,
      Tomato Julienne, Mustard Greens and Tarragon in
      Sherry Cream Sauce from Saracen....................130
McClellanville Crab Cakes with Sweet Red
      Pepper Cream from 82 Queen............................68
Mussels Marianne from Marianne.......................93
Oysters Elizabeth from 82 Queen........................67
Oysters with Thyme from Saracen.......................128
Pan Seared Grouper & Mussels from
      The Pinckney Cafe.......................................115
Risotto with Local Shellfish and Mushrooms
      from Louis's Charleston Grill..........................78
Scallops Sautéed in Bacon from The VarietyStore......145
Shrimp Alfredo fromBocci's...............................41
Shrimp and Grits from Tommy Condon's...............140
Shrimp Creole from Ronnie's.............................125
Shrimp Fried Rice from A.W. Shuck's...................23
Shrimp Newberg from A.W. Shuck's.....................23
Shrimp Paste from St. Andrew's Tea Room 134
Spicy Shrimp and Sausage over Creamy White Grits
      from Magnolia's...82

Page

Toogoodoo Vegetables and Shrimp in Parchment Paper
    from 82 Queen..69
To Boil Crabs from St. Andrew's Tea Room...........135
To Boil Shrimp from St. Andrew's Tea Room 135
To Fry Shrimp from St. Andrew's Tea Room..........135

SOUPS

Black Bean Soup form Alexander's.........................17
Confederate Bean Soup from Moultrie Tavern..........108
Charleston 13 Bean Soup from Hyman's.................73
Lemon Thyme Broth from the Village Cafe..............151
Mediterranean Vegetable Soup from Beaumont's........32
Okra Gumbo from Middleton Place Restaurant..........102
Seafood Chowder from Ronnie's.........................124
She Crab Soup from Middleton Place Restaurant........103
Sweet Pepper, Roasted Corn and Blue Crab Soup fro
    the Village Cafe..150

VEGETABLES

Carolina Grits from Carolina's.............................49
Fried Green Tomatoes from Carolina's....................49
Hoppin' John from Middleton Place Tea Room..........105
Lowcountry Collard Greens from Alexander's............18
Ratatouille from Marianne..................................90
Sweet Potato Soufflé from Bessinger's...................37
Zucchini E.B.T.C. from The East Bay
    Trading Company...59

Dear Reader,

We would appreciate your comments on DOIN' THE CHARLESTON. We have tried to make this little book one you will enjoy now and treasure later.

So please write! We'd like to respond. We are interested in your suggestions, ideas and impressions for use in our next edition.

Kindly address your letters and notes to me at our new home address in Nashville, Tenn.

If you wish an autographed copy, we'd be happy to oblidge. First send $13.95 and your full address to: Molly Keady Sillers
213 Haverford Drive
Nashville, Tenn. 37205